Mrs Green's Kettle
and other
Lincolnshire Acquittals

Mrs Green's Kettle and other Lincolnshire Acquittals

Malcolm Moyes

Copyright © 2023 Malcolm Moyes

The moral right of the author has been asserted.

Apart from any fair dealing for the purposes of research or private study, or criticism or review, as permitted under the Copyright, Designs and Patents Act 1988, this publication may only be reproduced, stored or transmitted, in any form or by any means, with the prior permission in writing of the publishers, or in the case of reprographic reproduction in accordance with the terms of licences issued by the Copyright Licensing Agency. Enquiries concerning reproduction outside those terms should be sent to the publishers.

Matador
Unit E2 Airfield Business Park,
Harrison Road, Market Harborough,
Leicestershire. LE16 7UL
Tel: 0116 2792299
Email: books@troubador.co.uk
Web: www.troubador.co.uk/matador
Twitter: @matadorbooks

ISBN 978 1803135 748

British Library Cataloguing in Publication Data.
A catalogue record for this book is available from the British Library.

Printed and bound by CPI Group (UK) Ltd, Croydon, CR0 4YY
Typeset in 12pt Minion Pro by Troubador Publishing Ltd, Leicester, UK

Matador is an imprint of Troubador Publishing Ltd

'What is Truth? Said jesting Pilate, and would not stay for an answer.
Francis Bacon, Of Truth (1625)

Contents

Acknowledgements	ix
Preface	xi
Chapter One: Jane Bell	1
Chapter Two: Elizabeth Dodds	42
Chapter Three: Ellen Green	111
Bibliography	192

Acknowledgements

I would like to thank the British Library which, through its digital archives of C19th and C20th newspapers, enabled me to access with relative ease the news reports and articles relating to the trials of Jane Bell, Elizabeth Dodds and Ellen Green, as well as their aftermath.

My thanks are also due to the staff of Sleaford and Lincoln libraries for their invaluable support in providing access to material in their local history collections, as well as obtaining scarce out of print books through the inter-library loan system.

Finally, I would like to thank the staff of the Lincolnshire Archives for their unfailing help and courtesy in giving me access to the various documents in their collections.

Preface

A search on the internet for information about the trials and tribulations of Jane Bell, Elizabeth Dodds and Ellen Green produces very little. In contrast, a similar search for information on Eliza Joyce, Mary Ann Milner and Priscilla Biggadike provides a good deal of information, some of it reliable, some less so.

All six women, between 1844 and 1875, were put on trial charged with administering fatal doses of arsenic to a member or members of their own family. Three of them were acquitted of the crime, the other three were found guilty and sentenced to be hanged.

Whilst it would not be difficult to explain the apparent lack of modern interest in the cases of the women who were acquitted, mainly in terms of the apparent lack of sensation, controversy and high drama, a convincing explanation of the reasons for their acquittal is less so.

A key problem was unintentionally highlighted

in the opening paragraph of the report on the trial of Ellen Green by the *Lincolnshire Chronicle* on the 30th July, 1875. The newspaper referred to the fact that Mrs Green had been arraigned purely on circumstantial evidence not dissimilar to that which had resulted in the execution of Priscilla Biggadike in 1868. The newspaper did not elaborate on its passing comment and it may be that the comparison, prefacing a lengthy report on a murder trial, was merely intended to encourage morbid curiosity and unhealthy speculation in its readers. More charitably, given that the reporter already knew the outcome of the trial of Ellen Green, he may have just sympathetically wished to remind the reader of the fact that the jury which had found Mrs Biggadike guilty of murder, also recommended mercy on the grounds that the conviction was based purely upon the circumstantial.

On the surface, the claim of similarities between the Green and Biggadike cases seems a reasonable one.

In both trials, the evidence against the two women consisted of hostile witness statements mainly drawn from unguarded conversations, which sometimes hinted at moral impropriety and marital difficulties, and so supplied a motive for the brutal killing of a husband. In both cases also, the alleged paramour of each of the accused married women was a suspect in the police investigation, but the bill against them was thrown out by a Grand Jury, and the two men were therefore conveniently enabled to give evidence against the accused in court.

The two women also concocted quite ludicrous exculpatory stories which were clearly untrue and contradictory, and which were later used against them in court to undermine their credibility, as well as their moral character.

On the other hand, there were also significant differences between the two sets of circumstantial evidence in the cases. Mrs Biggadike claimed that she had tasted the poisoned medicine intended for her husband and was ill over the next few days, yet nobody ever witnessed her being sick. Mrs Green also had claimed to have ingested arsenic and had been made ill by it: several witnesses affirmed the truth of her vomiting, although three medical experts expressed a good deal of scepticism about Mrs Green's rapid recovery and the nature of her sickness: it was certainly an area vigorously contested by the Counsel for the Prosecution.

Whilst both Richard Biggadike and Thomas Green died from arsenic poisoning, the issues of ownership of the poison, the reasons for its purchase and its whereabouts at the time of its supposed administration to the victim were very different. A search of the Biggadike house for arsenic by the police drew a blank and the Counsel for the Prosecution had to rely upon the questionable memory of a witness having wanted to borrow some poison from Priscilla Biggadike, although without ever having either seen or received it. In addition, the two lodgers at the Biggadike residence, George Ironmonger and Thomas Proctor, both claimed that they had never seen any arsenic in the house during the time they had lived there.

A thorough search of the household of Mrs Green discovered ample quantities of arsenic in various unusual places, but it was accounted for in terms of the poison having been previously used by Mr Green to deal with vermin and that he had disposed of what he had not used, probably somewhere in the garden.

In the final analysis, the point being made by the reporter, whilst containing some truth, could easily have been applied to many other cases of alleged husband poisoning in the mid-C19th, both in and beyond the county, given the secret and insidious nature of the crime and the often paper-thin, flimsy nature of the circumstantial.

Whatever the intention of the *Lincolnshire Chronicle* newspaper, the comparison does raise serious questions concerning the consistency of the judicial system, and the extent to which it was fit for purpose in such capital crimes. It also invites the identification of other significant factors beyond the accumulated vagaries of circumstantial evidence which might account for the kind of inconsistency and inadequacy implied by the reporter.

The question is not whether the verdict was correct, but how and why it was reached, and by whom.

By virtue of his social and professional prestige in a deferential society and his privileged position in the structure of a capital trial, the views of the judge were, without question, potentially crucial in determining any outcome. The formulaic utterance from the Bench that the final verdict was purely in the hands of the jury created a convenient and comforting illusion about the fairness of the jury system, rather than an accurate reflection of reality. It is quite clear that despite assurances to the contrary, judges were not always impartial and even-handed adjudicators, but like everyone else in the courtroom were subject to personal prejudices, some petty, shaped by age, background and life experiences, as well as by legal precedent.

In his introductory remarks put before a Grand Jury concerning the Calendar, the judge evaluated the relative seriousness of the alleged crimes and in so doing offered clear guidance on the merits of the individual charges. Such advice was informed by him having considered and reflected at length upon the depositions and was given additional weight by his experience and professional status. A Grand Jury might disagree with the guidance, and sometimes did, but it would require sound reasoning or assured self-confidence to do so.

Once the trial of a serious crime was underway, after a true bill had been found, and the competing Counsels were doing their best to prove the case either for or against the accused, the judge had the power to make unscheduled interventions. Such interventions were intended to clarify depositions or rule on a point of law, but the very act of intervention, especially when challenging a witness, was potentially a re-directioning, intentional or otherwise, of a jury's thoughts and opinions.

Perhaps the most powerful and decisive intervention by the judge was his summing up of the case before the jury retired. Its intention was to provide an objective overview of the evidence and the issues arising from that evidence, which the jury should consider. Given the volume of the evidence, made more complex by the subtle and sometimes not so subtle arguments presented by the two Counsels, the task of impartially selecting and summarising was a formidable one. The reported length of some judicial summaries intended to support the jury in the decision-making process underlined the hazardous and challenging nature of the task. In the view of James Fitzjames Stephen, arguably one of the sharpest legal minds of the nineteenth-century, the very act of selecting and ordering the evidence to establish the essential relationships between the constituent parts of the case in itself inevitably pointed to a particular conclusion. In summing up a case which was unclear and in which the two Counsels had been evenly matched, the problem of a loss of objectivity and consequent judicial partisanship became especially acute, as the judge tried his best to guide a struggling jury. In view of the impossibility of total objectivity in the process of summing up, it is not surprising that Stephen suggested that a judge should not even attempt to conceal his personal opinions from a jury.

Further, it is clear from the language and emphases of some of the reported summaries voiced by the Learned Judge that they were nothing less than an undisguised attempt to push a jury towards a particular verdict. Indeed, some legal commentators of the time thought it was an acceptable part of the legal process for a judge to influence a jury into making what he thought to be the right decision.

A close analysis of the summary of Mr Justice Byles at the end of the trial of Priscilla Biggadike, for example, at times reads like a sustained attempt to manoeuvre the jury into a preferred outcome, rather than being a balanced presentation of the issues. The undisguised antipathy of Sir John Gurney towards prisoners in general, amounting to a callous personal vendetta, was the stuff of legend, which even made some of his learned friends uncomfortable.

Because the judge had a very public voice in a trial, the media often reported his words in detail, if not always accurately, which created a sense of him being the most influential factor in the outcome of trial. Conversely, the voice of the jury, by the very nature of the process, received no such coverage beyond the occasional question and the formulaic response of a verdict which concluded their participation.

The function of a jury is to a reach a decision after listening to and evaluating evidence and arguments presented by the witnesses as well as by the judge. Common sense, therefore, suggests that the key factor in determining the outcome of a trial is a jury: that was their purpose and their civic duty, after all.

How and why a particular decision was reached by a nineteenth-century jury after it retired, however, is almost impossible to assess with any accuracy in the absence of a record of the discussion. It becomes even more problematic when the jury arrived at a verdict in less than ten minutes and sometimes without even moving out of the jury box – an outrage which in part gave rise to Alexander Pope's much quoted barbed couplet from Canto 3 of *The Rape of the Lock*, lines 21-22:

*The hungry judges soon the sentence sign
And wretches hang that jurymen may dine.*

Even if a set of Minutes of the jury's deliberations existed, any sense of the interplay between the individual jurors, which might have determined the direction of the final verdict, would remain purely speculative. The power of Sidney Lumet's 1957 film, *12 Angry Men,* is its dramatization of such discussions and arguments by the jurors, as well as the dynamics of personal agendas which shape and determine the outcome of a trial. Over seventy years later, the significance of such jury dynamics was still seen as a powerful dramatic tool, explored during the trial of Helen Titchener at Borchester Crown Court for the murder of her husband, in BBC Radio 4's popular series *The Archers.*

The responsibility for the final verdict, in capital crimes, was an awesome one which determined the life or death of the accused, as Defence Counsels were always keen to remind a jury in their summing up. It was also a decision which the jurors would have to live with for the rest of their lives and should therefore be made, in the memorable phrase of Sir John Compton Lawrance at the trial of Mary Lefley, 'in merciful consideration of themselves'.

The jury might have to live with the decision, as well as with any hostile responses of the general public to that decision, but they had no opportunity to explain it. The judge, on the other hand, was able to reflect upon and explain the verdict of the jury, usually in clichéd pejorative terms of shock and horror at the enormity of the crime, before putting on his black cap and offering the cold comfort of a prison Chaplain's spiritual instruction to the condemned.

Whilst it is difficult to accurately work out the extent to which the jury reached its verdict independent of the judicial summing up, it is possible, at least, to assess the competence of a jury to reach a just decision, as well as its ability to resist the direction of the judge, should it be required.

Members of the jury in capital crimes were listed in newspaper reports, and by virtue of their wealth and social status were usually well known influential public figures, such Lord John Monson, Charles Chaplin and Sir Charles Anderson, in Lincolnshire. They were also often well known to each other, by way of political, economic and social links, as well as by previous jury service. As well educated men, experienced in terms of making difficult decisions as magistrates and following the intricacies of lengthy expositions, fine distinctions and convoluted debate which unfolded in committee rooms, they were well placed to reach a considered and balanced verdict. Several members of the jury in the trials of the six women in question were either serving MPs or former

MPs for various parts of Lincolnshire, and therefore experienced in decoding the rhetoric of public debate. In a sense, as men in the public eye, it was also in their interest to be seen to have reached a considered and balanced verdict, in terms of local reputation and enhanced confidence in their judgement.

It might be argued, of course, that the shared privileged background of such jurors, living important lives in impressive residences, compared to the obscure, ordinary and sometimes squalid lives of the accused, might have produced a casual indifference to the fate of the feckless. A line of least resistance to an unambiguous summing up by a Learned Judge was sometimes perhaps preferable to answering uncomfortable retrospective questions and having to justify any disturbance to an unforgiving status quo, seemingly obsessed by frightful thoughts of unchecked criminality. The power of the shared values of social stability and the function of the law as a fearful deterrent would ultimately win any delicate arguments about the relationship between poverty and criminality, no matter how liberal-minded and well-intentioned the juror.

On the other hand, elements of diversity in a jury may have prevented deliberations from being the easy consensus of an echo chamber and influence the final outcome. The divergent political outlooks of the Conservative and Liberal jurors concerning the first principles of social justice, for example, at least had the potential to generate constructive conflict in a debate about the reliability of evidence. Even so staunch an advocate of retaining the death penalty as James Fitzjames Stephen was compelled to admit in front of the Royal Commission on Capital Punishment of 1865-66 that if there was anyone on the jury in a capital trial who objected to the death sentence it 'might make a difference' to the verdict.

The composition of juries dominated by such highly respected gentlemen as Charles Allix of West Willoughby Hall and John Lewis Ffytche of Thorpe Hall, would probably have given confidence in their judgements and in their ability to do the job. However, juries which consisted mainly of successful small farmers and shopkeepers who lacked the professional experience and skill sets to meet the complex demands of jury service, were perhaps less likely to enjoy that confidence.

The description of a day, sometimes days, spent in court with few comforts was described by Herbert Ibbetson, the radical Manchester solicitor and founder of the National Jury System Reform Association, as 'painfully disagreeable'. In general, the thrust of his polemic was against the shabby way in which jurors were treated by a system which compelled them to give up their time and services free of charge. What was also a matter of concern was jury sequestration during the course of a long trial and having to endure conditions which were conducive to neither good will nor sound judgement the following day. Whilst the extended inconveniences and discomforts of the jury in the sensational trial of the Rugeley poisoner, William Palmer, at the Old Bailey, in 1856, were exceptional, less infamous examples also highlighted the issue as an urgent one. At the Lincoln Lent Assizes of 1863, for example, during the trial of John and Elizabeth Garner, the so-called Mareham le Fen poisoners, a jury was locked up overnight in a local hotel without beds and with very little food. The unsatisfactory arrangements were later acknowledged by the trial judge, Mr Justice Willes, who offered to fine the Under-Sherriff £20 for his negligence – compensation which was later changed to £10 on the generous intervention of the Foreman of the Jury, who blamed the landlord of the hotel for the shambles. The unfortunate farce also provided the defeated Counsel for the Prosecution, some years later, with the excuse that the exhausted state of the jury had made them unfit to hear the case, ultimately leading to a verdict of manslaughter, rather than wilful murder: in the view of the crestfallen lawyer, the inadequate and uncivilised care for the jury had led to a serious miscarriage of justice.

On a more mundane practical level, the ends of justice were not best served by jurors who had the inconvenience of travelling to Lincoln at their own expense from such far-flung edges of the county as Fleet Hargate and Crowland. Even more dispiriting, a trial lasting the entire day, and sometimes beyond, conducted in a language at times elusive, would not have been the most effective remedy against a lack of sustained concentration and minds wandering towards more pressing issues, such as the impact of the weather on crops that day or an unexpected downturn in trade the previous week.

The 1861 painting by John Morgan titled *The Jury*, gently satiric in its depiction of distraction and indifference in an Aylesbury courtroom, captures such uncomfortable commonplace realities for a jury consisting of men who would rather be elsewhere.

Whilst the extending of civic duty beyond a small elite of the wealthy and powerful was a worthy development in the C19th democratic project, it left inexperienced juries vulnerable to such public blunders as that of the Foreman of the Jury in the Priscilla Biggadike trial, thinking that a recommendation for mercy could be justified by referring to the uncertainties of circumstantial evidence: a naivety ridiculed and lambasted by the *Montrose Standard* of the 18th December, 1868, which bluntly declared that, 'The sooner criminals are tried for their lives by rational beings instead of idiots the better'.

As the nineteenth-century progressed, courtrooms more and more became a theatre for the performance of rhetorical tricks, in which the Learned Counsels made or marred their professional reputations. The judge might have the advantage of the first and last word at an Assize trial, as well as having the right to intervene during the course of the proceedings, but a bravura performance from a professional lawyer, could influence both a judge, should he be open to persuasion, and the gentlemen of the jury. The importance of the power of both the Counsel for the Defence and the Prosecution was increasingly recognised by newspaper reporters who saw them as key players in the unfolding courtroom drama recreated for the entertainment and instruction of their readers. The brief clichéd compliment of 'a powerful and eloquent speech' evolved into a detailed record of the words spoken at the beginning and end of the trial, with their skilful mix of detached observation, sharp analysis and emotive pleading which swayed the verdict for or against the accused.

Jane Bell, Elizabeth Dodds and Ellen Green were all found Not Guilty. In the case of Mrs Bell, the verdict was reached and nothing more was heard of the matter; the acquittal of Mrs Dodds was the subject of an outraged article in a London newspaper and a passing mention in the Royal Commission on Capital Punishment, before being quietly consigned to the status of a judicial statistic; Mrs Green, on the other hand, was less fortunate in that her exoneration provoked threats of mob violence against her in the streets of Lincoln and merciless scorn in the popular press.

An explanation of Jane Bell's acquittal is probably rooted in an accumulation of different factors, rather than just the shortcomings of circumstantial evidence.

From the outset of the judicial process, there was clearly a good deal of doubt about her guilt, expressed in the cautious inconclusive verdict of a Coroner's court. Even after the uncovering of supposed new evidence pointing towards Mrs Bell being guilty of murder and leading to her being sent for trial at the Assize court by the magistrates, there seemed little of substance upon which the Prosecution might construct a convincing case.

The Grand Jury on the day was an experienced panel which was always unlikely to be persuaded by evidence which failed to produce a credible motive and whose main source was a witness whose testimony was rooted in less than worthy motives.

In addition, it is possible that Mrs Bell's pregnancy elicited the emotional sympathy of the Grand Jury from the outset, as well as a more rational uneasy awareness of the implications of finding her Guilty of a capital crime.

Curiously, one of the jurors, Richard Thorald, was

the presiding magistrate who had sent Jane Bell to Lincoln for trial in the first place: he seemed to have been persuaded to change his mind after seventeen minutes of discussion.

There was no courtroom drama involving contending Counsels as the accused had no legal representation. The flatness of the trial was perhaps reflected in the newspaper reports which made little mention of the Prosecuting Counsel, Mr Wildsmith, other than him being present in court and conducting the case.

The final verdict of Not Guilty, however, was probably less to do with the quality of the evidence, than an insistently sympathetic reading of a principle of law by the judge. The directioning of Mr Justice Mawle, who from the outset did little to hide his views, erred on the side of caution in favour of the accused. In the opening address to the Grand Jury, he insisted that if there was any doubt about the guilt of a prisoner, he or she should be given the benefit of that doubt. It was an assertion which he repeated in his summing up of the case, before the Grand Jury retired to deliberate. Whilst the Press reported that the Learned Judge delivered a lengthy consideration of the case, its main focus was upon his unambiguous view that he had heard nothing to connect the prisoner directly to the crime, and concluded by repeating his advice about sufficient doubt.

If there was a distinct lack of courtroom drama in the case of Jane Bell, the opposite was true in the trial of Elizabeth Dodds. The circumstantial evidence relating to the means, the opportunity and the motive for murder, rooted in marital disharmony, seemed convincing. It required either a poor performance by the Counsel for the Prosecution or an exceptional one by the Counsel for the Defence to save Mrs Dodds from the hangman: it got both.

In his opening remarks to the Grand Jury, the presiding judge, Baron Bramwell, was measured and scrupulously impartial. Whilst being somewhat alarmed at there being four cases of alleged murder to consider, he was restrained in his observations: even the case of Thomas Richardson, accused of shooting a policeman in Wyberton and the only prisoner to be eventually found guilty, was described fairly and objectively.

Similarly, the facts of the matter relating to the case of Elizabeth Dodds, were described without prejudice: Mrs Dodds had without doubt bought poison which had killed her husband, so the question for the Grand Jury was the reason for buying it. The Grand Jury clearly thought that there was enough evidence to find a true bill against Mrs Dodds and she was put on trial for wilful murder. By definition, at this point in the judicial process, the Grand Jury entertained thoughts of a Guilty verdict.

Baron Bramwell's final summary of the case, as reported by the *Lincolnshire Chronicle* and the *Stamford Mercury*, was similarly even-handed, reviewing the salient points of the evidence 'in a clear and most impartial manner'. The short quotation from the judge's summary, with its scrupulously balanced parallel clauses, as reported by the *Stamford Mercury*, captured the sense that the verdict really had been left entirely in the capable hands of the jury: 'It would be a very shocking thing to say the prisoner was guilty, and then forfeit her life, when she was innocent of the crime; and it would be equally shocking for a jury to say she was not guilty, when the evidence showed her to be so'.

The Grand Jury had many such experienced and capable hands, including three Members of Parliament and two former Members of Parliament, but that was no guarantee of a Not Guilty verdict, of course. The circumstantial evidence against Mrs Dodds was strong, much of it having its origins in damning conversations with close friends and neighbours, including her lodger, and rumours of marital dissension. The Grand Jury would have to be persuaded by convincing arguments from the Counsel for the Defence in order to remove its most serious doubts about the innocence of Mrs Dodds.

The reporter from the *Stamford Mercury* clearly realised that the performance of the Counsel for the

Defence during the course of the hearing and the closing speech had been a crucial factor in swaying the jury towards a verdict of Not Guilty. Reported in verbatim detail, the closing speech of the Counsel for the Defence, with its forensic attention to the language of the depositions, its application of common sense to suspicious trains of events and the well-judged undermining of witnesses, seemed to confirm its decisive influence on the outcome of the trial.

The case for the Defence was helped by the underperformance of the Counsel for the Prosecution who appeared to be poorly briefed, too dependent upon the weight of medical evidence to clinch the case and perhaps too complacent to sharpen up his presentation of the strongest evidence to the jury.

A key factor in the acquittal of Ellen Green is more difficult to determine with any confidence.

There was a bewildering array of witnesses for the jury to hear, some of who contradicted other witnesses and sometimes even themselves; the narratives deposed by the accused were scarcely credible, but were supported by her sister and a dying declaration from her husband, whom she may or may not have poisoned; and the alleged paramour of Mrs Green, John Bonnett, who was in a position to clarify a number of important issues, instead chose to impress the public gallery with his talents as a bawdy comic raconteur.

The presiding judge, Mr Justice Lindley, drew attention to the case of Mrs Green, after advising the Grand Jury that they need not consider the other serious case of Peter Blanchard, as a true bill had been found against him at the previous Assize session. The no nonsense judge briefly described the circumstances of the case without any kind of bias, although he seemed slightly bemused that the Prosecution had claimed that Mrs Green had put arsenic in a kettle.

In his summing up of the case, he seemed equally bemused, finding a lack of credibility in the various contradictory narratives concerning who had administered the poison, which he had listened to during the course of the day.

After having had to contend with unseemly and boisterous behaviour in the public gallery, whilst having to follow the twisting uncertainties of an almost intractable case, perhaps His Lordship was relieved that the final decision was in the hands of a capable Grand Jury.

The two Counsels, Mr Stephen and Mr Lawrance, both men of experience in such difficult trials, had presented coherent narratives of what may or may not have taken place in Fishtoft on the morning of the 17th May, 1875, but seemingly had not convinced Justice Lindley one way or the other.

It appears that the same might be said of the

Grand Jury, which took two hours to reach a Not Guilty verdict.

It is probable that like his Lordship, the jury was not absolutely convinced by the reconstructed narratives of either guilt or innocence.

It may be that the gentlemen of the jury, sensitive to the reputation of the county, reached their verdict, not on the grounds of credible evidence and arguments, but on a wish to avoid a decision which would have meant the passing of a second death sentence in four days, following the trial and condemnation of Peter Blanchard.

Chapter One

Jane Bell (1808-?)

Jane Bell: Timeline

13th May, 1829: marriage of Jane Cooling to Edward Bell at St Denys' Church, Killingholme.

14th - 26th March, 1845: Edward Bell attended by Dr H M Leppington.

25th March, 1845: Jane Bell purchases a quantity of arsenic from the shop of Horace Watson in Laceby.

26th March, 1845: death of Edward Bell, aged forty-one, from suspected arsenic poisoning, leaving his wife, aged thirty-seven, with three children: Mary aged thirteen, George, aged eleven and Sarah Jane, aged three, as well with the care of her elderly pauper mother, Faith Cooling, aged seventy-seven.

28th March, 1845: inquest into the death of Edward Bell at Waterloo Inn, Laceby, before Coroner, George Marris: adjourned.

: Jane Bell held in custody.

2nd April, 1845: resumed inquest into the death of Edward Bell at Waterloo Inn. Verdict of Coroner's jury inconclusive. Jane Bell released.

5th April, 1845: warrant issued by magistrate: Jane Bell rearrested and taken to Grimsby gaol.

6th April, 1845: Jane Bell remanded in custody in Grimsby by magistrate, accused of the wilful murder of her husband.

7th April, 1845: hearing in Magistrates' Court, Grimsby: Jane Bell sent for trial at Lincoln Assizes. Taken back to Grimsby gaol.

8th April, 1845: incarceration of Jane Bell in Lincoln Castle gaol.

22nd July, 1845: trial of Jane Bell at Lincoln Assizes in front of the Right Honourable Sir William Henry Mawle. Found Not Guilty by a Grand Jury and acquitted.

'I Have Nothing Else To Say': The Acquittal of Jane Bell

The story of the poisoning of Edward Bell by his wife, Jane Bell, at Laceby, just over four miles from Grimsby, was first reported by the *Lincolnshire Chronicle* and the *Stamford Mercury*, on the 4th April, 1845. It was a story which fed into a larger national narrative, rife in the 1840s, that the country was enduring an epidemic of murder by arsenic poisoning.

The two very brief reports recorded the death of Edward Bell and a subsequent inquest, but provided little detail beyond the discovery of arsenic by the post mortem examination and the detaining of Jane Bell in custody on suspicion of administering the poison. Both newspapers ended their short reports somewhat perfunctorily: the *Stamford Mercury* apologised that it could not give the reader more information as the Coroner's jury had not reached a decision 'when our correspondent's letter was closed'; whilst the *Lincolnshire Chronicle* promised more details in the following week's publication, for the same reason.

Both newspapers resumed the story on the 11th April, but both remained disappointingly limited in their presentation of a lucid and coherent account of the case.

The *Stamford Mercury* was vague and unhelpfully brief in its report, beginning in the middle of the case with the appearance of Mrs Bell in front of the Grimsby magistrates, Richard Thorald and the Reverend Joseph Gedge, on the 6th April, having been charged with administering poison to her husband, from which 'he became violently sick and died'. A number of medical witnesses had provided evidence of the presence of sufficient arsenic in the body of the deceased to cause death, whilst 'another witness' had testified that Mrs Bell had purchased a quantity of arsenic 'under the pretence of killing bugs'. Whilst the evidence was purely circumstantial, it was sufficient to satisfy both magistrates of her guilt, and Jane Bell was committed for trial at Lincoln. The thumbnail report ended by stating that Mrs Bell was pregnant at the time and also that she strongly denied the charge.

The report in the *Lincolnshire Chronicle* with the headline 'Death from Poison', was much longer than that of the *Stamford Mercury*, but also gave the impression that it either did not know, or chose not to publish, some essentials of the story which the reader might have found helpful, in particular, those relating to the initial inquest and its aftermath, which had been hastily reported the week before.

The report unexpectedly began with the resumed inquest at the Waterloo Inn, Laceby, into the death of Edward Bell, which had taken place on the previous Wednesday, 2nd April. After the recapitulation of the evidence and considered deliberation by the

Coroner's jury, a verdict of wilful murder by person or persons unknown had been reached. As a result, Jane Bell, who had been in custody at the time, was released.

Unfortunately for Mrs Bell, on the following Saturday, she was taken back into custody at Grimsby gaol, under an arrest warrant issued by the magistrates acting for the parts of Lindsey. Her acquittal at the Coroner's Court had left the authorities dissatisfied and they had therefore launched further enquiries into the circumstances of Edward Bell's death, on the basis of his wife's 'previous suspicious behaviour' and the evidence presented to the inquest jury.

On the Sunday morning, Mrs Bell was conducted from gaol by two constables to the magistrate's office on Haven Street, and remanded until the following day. In an attempt to add colour to the plain facts, the newspaper reported that Mrs Bell had been followed by a large number of people 'anxious to get a sight of her'. The reporter's human interest story continued with an apparently sympathetic description of the prisoner. Her facial expressions indicated a good deal of bodily discomfort, which the reporter attributed to 'her unhappy situation' and also to the fact of her being pregnant.

On the Sunday evening, Mrs Bell was 'taken violently ill' and was treated by the Grimsby surgeon, Mr Leppington, who provided some relief for her distress. In passing, the reporter mentioned that a similar attack had taken place on a previous occasion, when Mrs Bell was in custody at Laceby. It is difficult to work out whether the information was offered in sympathy or as a cynical aside suggesting a degree of theatrical duplicity by Jane Bell.

On the Monday morning, 7th April, Mrs Bell appeared in front of the two magistrates and was charged with the wilful murder of her husband by administering arsenic poison.

The *Lincolnshire Chronicle* supplied some information relating to the depositions before the magistrates, although it remained highly selective in its choice of witness statements and the detail in which they were reported.

A post mortem on the body of Edward Bell had been carried out at the initial inquest in Laceby by the two Grimsby surgeons, Mr Leppington and Mr Bell, along with an assistant Mr Keetley, which had clearly and decisively reached the conclusion of death by arsenic poisoning. Their opinion had been later corroborated by Mr Pearsall, a consulting chemist of Hull, who had conducted a chemical examination of the stomach of Edward Bell, along with Mr Leppington and Mr Bell. It was satisfactorily proven that the quantity of arsenic discovered in the stomach was sufficient to cause death.

Mr Horace Watson, druggist of Laceby, and

probably the person unhelpfully referred to by the *Stamford Mercury* as 'another witness' was the next to give evidence. Mr Watson deposed that the prisoner had bought arsenic from his shop just before the death of her husband, allegedly to kill vermin. He added that according to Mrs Bell she had not used the arsenic, but had thrown it away.

At this point, the *Lincolnshire Chronicle* becomes as vague as the *Stamford Mercury*. There were several other witnesses whose evidence 'strongly attached guilt to the prisoner', but no details were supplied by the newspaper. The omission was somewhat disingenuously justified through a lack of space: the other depositions were too numerous and lengthy to report. The reader was reassured, however, that the evidence against Mrs Bell was 'so strong and conclusive as to justify the magistrates in committing the prisoner to Lincoln to take her trial'.

The newspaper further reported Jane Bell's denial of the charge after being invited to offer a defence. Mrs Bell clearly thought that there was very little to say on account of her being totally innocent of the crime. She briefly stated her version of the facts relating to her husband's illness and her purchase of the arsenic, before declaring, 'I have nothing else to say, I am as clear of my husband's death as the child that I am in the family with'.

According to the newspaper, the prisoner wept

bitterly on being removed from the magistrates' office and was transported to Lincoln in a chaise the following day.

The report of the case of Jane Bell, published by the *Evening Standard*, on the 14th April, and several other London newspapers on the same day, occasionally clarifies some of the vagaries and omissions of the two Lincolnshire newspapers.

Despite a couple of misspellings amounting to misnomers, elevating Edward Bell from a higgler into a master carter and relocating the Grimsby surgeons to Laceby, the *Evening Standard* provided useful information from the initial inquest.

The opening of the report tapped into the national mood: 'Another of those shocking acts of poisoning which of late have been a too frequent occurrence in the country, has recently come to light at a small village called Laceby, near Grimsby'. The wife of the victim, Jane Bell, had been committed to Lincoln Castle for trial, charged with the murder of her husband, Edward Bell, who had died suddenly on the 26th March.

Bell was generally considered to be in a good state of health at the time of his death and so a County Coroner, Mr Marris, had been required to conduct an inquest at the Waterloo Inn, at Laceby, on the 28th March, in order to investigate any suspicious circumstances.

Mr Marris first heard depositions from Mr Leppington and Mr Keetley, based upon their post mortem examination and careful examination of the stomach. Satisfied that the deceased had died from 'the powerful effects of arsenic', and also alerted to 'other suspicious facts, tending to fix upon the unhappy woman the commission of the shocking act', the Coroner ordered Mrs Bell to be taken into the custody of the 'proper authorities'.

At which point, the inquest was adjourned to allow for further investigation and the collection of fresh evidence concerning 'the tragical event'.

At the resumption of the inquest, it was suggested that the arsenic had been administered in arrowroot; additional evidence had also been uncovered which incriminated Mrs Bell, although the newspaper did not provide any specific details. Despite the discovery of new evidence, however, the jury had remained unconvinced that it was sufficient to charge Jane Bell.

As reported in the *Lincolnshire Chronicle*, the liberation of Mrs Bell was short-lived, as she was re-apprehended on the strength of evidence of her behaviour towards her husband which had already been heard at the Coroner's court and the further enquiries into the 'mysterious affair'.

The account of the incarceration of Mrs Bell and her appearance in front of the magistrates, like the *Lincolnshire Chronicle*, emphasised her insistence of being innocent, although presented a much more dramatic account of her emotional turmoil. She was about five months pregnant and wept bitterly throughout the proceedings; she also was reported as frequently exclaiming, 'I am clear of my husband's death. I did not cause it'.

Trial of Jane Bell at The Lincoln Assizes, 22nd July, 1845

The Lincoln Summer Assizes opened on Saturday, 19th July, preceded by the usual civic fanfare reserved for visiting judges. Sir William Frederick Pollock, a university friend of the poet Tennyson, and the Right Honourable Sir William Henry Mawle were met by the High Sheriff of Lincoln, Thomas Coltman, at the South Bar Gate, and escorted to their lodgings.

The Grand Jury was elected and consisted of the following:

- Right Honourable Lord Worsely, MP (Foreman)
- Charles Allix
- Charles Henry John Anderson
- Ayscough Boucherett
- John Bromhead
- Francis Brown
- Charles Chaplin
- Thomas Chaplin

- Robert Adam Christopher MP
- Thomas George Corbett
- Robert Cracroft
- John Fardell
- John Lewis Ffytche
- William Hutton
- Theophilus Fairfax Johnson
- Charles B Luard
- Charles Mainwaring
- George Hussey Packe
- John Reeve
- Gervaise Tottenham Waldo Sibthorp
- Richard Thorald
- Edward Wright
- John Whiting Yorke

The opening remarks of Justice Mawle to the Grand Jury were unusually relaxed: whilst there were a couple of cases which were of a very serious nature, he did not think that they called for any particular comment from him. The learned judge did not identify the cases by name, but he was almost certainly referring to the alleged murder of William Parks at Skellingthorpe by William Graham and the alleged poisoning of Edward Bell at Laceby, by Jane Bell. However, should the Grand Jury require his assistance, his Lordship would be very happy to give it. In his view, in very serious cases, it would be more desirable to find no true bill, unless a conviction was assured. He also warned that 'even very strong suspicion' was not sufficient to convict a prisoner and so finding a true bill might still lead to an acquittal, which in turn would defeat the ends of justice.

Despite his caveats, Lord Justice Mawle ended with the usual reassuring formula that in the final analysis, the verdict would be left in the capable hands of the jury.

The unruffled comments from his Lordship suggest that he thought the court's business would be relatively straightforward. To an extent he was correct, in that most of the alleged crimes were unexceptional and routine, involving the theft of sheep and horses, stabbing, burglary, forgery, violent robbery and concealing a birth. They were cases which would probably be forgotten by the time the judges departed for the next Assize session, and more of the same.

However, the prosecution of two of the felons was less than routine and may have stuck in the memory of his Lordship for some time.

The *Stamford Mercury* reported that Shropshire born Richard Brookfield was convicted of stealing three geese and an overcoat and was asked if there was anything he had to say before sentence was passed. An impenitent Mr Brookfield, it seems, had a good deal to say on the matter: 'I shall do it again; I will never work while there is anything in the country'. The reporter described Mr Brookfield as 'a very candid criminal'.

The court report found in the *Liverpool Mercury* of the 1st August and also published in the *Manchester Courier and Lancashire General Advertiser* the day after, provided an extended version of the incident. According to the two newspapers, Justice Mawle had been on the point of handing down a lenient sentence, when Richard Brookfield interrupted the judicial process with his sturdy declaration of intent to continue his criminal career. In addition, he advised his Lordship that 'you can do just as you please' when it came to passing sentence. Justice Mawle, unimpressed by the plucky, plain-speaking honesty of Mr Brookfield, did just that, replying, 'Then the sentence of the court is that you be transported for seven years. Perhaps that will satisfy you'. The prisoner left the dock laughing, on his way to Van Diemen's Land, courtesy of the *Mount Stewart Elphinstone* convict ship.

Luton man George Smith, with his accomplice George Folkes, from Long Sutton, was found guilty of breaking into the house of the farmer, William Reeson, at Leake, and was sentenced to be transported for ten years. The response of Mr Smith to his sentence was less overtly impertinent than that of Richard Brookfield, but no less unexpected: rather than protesting his innocence or disputing the harshness of the sentence, he merely said with barely disguised irony, 'thank you my Lord', and left the court to start his journey to Norfolk Island Penal Colony six months later, on board the *China*, alongside George Folkes and another one hundred and ninety-eight convicts. Even the *Stamford Mercury* was left speechless.

The trial of Jane Bell for murder contained no such comic episodes, at least not until the very end, when Justice Mawle confirmed his own reputation for ironic wit.

The story was reported at length by both the *Lincolnshire Chronicle* and the *Stamford Mercury*: both accounts were similar, with the odd additional piece of information, although their reporting of the statement made by Mrs Bell in her own defence contained significant differences.

The case for the Prosecution was conducted by Mr Richard Wildman, but the prisoner was undefended.

According to the report of the trial published in the *Hull Packet and East Riding Times*, Justice Mawle kindly asked that the pregnant Mrs Bell be provided with a chair, after which she seated herself 'composedly' and removed her bonnet.

Mr Hildyard Marshall Leppington, surgeon, was the first witness to depose. He had given evidence at the inquest into the death of Edward Bell and had confirmed death by arsenic poison. In his appearance at Lincoln, he gave a much more detailed account of his dealings with the deceased man which seemed to undermine any claim that he had been in robust good health at the time of his death.

The surgeon recalled that he had been asked to attend Edward Bell on the 14th March and had found him suffering from 'a congested state of the viscera of the abdomen, with a constriction of the bowels, and sickness'. He had continued to treat him until the 25th March, during which time he was 'a little better', although at the same time, he thought his patient 'might be in some danger': it was not the most convincing account of decisive and effective medical care.

Mr Leppington had visited the house again, on the 26th March, only to discover that Edward Bell had died. His first response had been to ask Mrs Bell if she had correctly administered her husband's medicine based on his 'directions', to which she replied in the affirmative, adding that his condition had deteriorated during the night. The follow up question posed to Mrs Bell was an unsubtle probing of the whereabouts of a quantity of arsenic: he had heard 'some reports' that she had purchased the poison only the day before. He was informed by Mrs Bell that she had mixed it with some chamber lye and had then placed it in an outbuilding.

Mr Leppington then moved away from anecdotal

evidence to the more comfortable and secure subject of human anatomy, reminding the jury that he had performed the post mortem and had assisted in the removal of the contents of the stomach. He had also taken the stomach to Mr Pearsall in Hull and was present when the tests were performed. The first test was carried out using ammonia sulphate of copper, which immediately indicated the presence of arsenic in the stomach. A similar result was obtained when Mr Pearsall applied ammonia nitrate of silver.

Mr Leppington told the court that after having carried out the post mortem, he had spoken to Mrs Bell, who had expressed the hope that 'he had found nothing which could lay anything to her charge'. He had assured her that 'justice would be done to (*sic*) her'.

John Bell, surgeon and apothecary of Grimsby, confirmed that he had assisted Mr Leppington with the post mortem, on the 28th March. He also deposed that he had spoken with Jane Bell, asking her a series of questions, some of them related to classic symptoms of arsenic poisoning. He first enquired whether her husband had complained of any particular symptoms during the night, to which she made no reply. He had then asked her if he had vomited, to which she replied, only after taking Mr Leppington's medicine. Asked if her husband had complained of a burning throat or raging thirst, she replied in the negative. Mrs Bell quite clearly did not make any significant contributions to the progress of medical jurisprudence in Lincolnshire.

Mr Bell returned to his part in the examination of the body of Edward Bell by telling the court that he had assisted in the putting of the stomach into a bladder, ready to be taken to Mr Pearsall in Hull. He also said that he had observed some gritty particles in the folds of the stomach, but had not investigated them, as the former analysis (presumably meaning that by Mr Pearsall), 'proved so satisfactory'. At this point, according to the *Stamford Mercury* only, the judge pressed the witness concerning how many stomachs suspected of containing arsenic he had examined in the past. In response, Mr Bell admitted that he had only ever seen one before: however, he was confident that Edward Bell had died from the ingestion of an irritant poison.

Thomas Bell Keetley, assistant to John Bell, had also helped in the post mortem examination and had also accompanied him to Hull to support Mr Pearsall in the conduct his chemical examination. From what he had observed, there could be no doubt that arsenic had been the immediate cause of death; further, in his estimation, it must have been a remarkably large dose.

The final medical expert to take the stand was Thomas John Pearsall himself whom the *Lincolnshire Chronicle* described as a 'lecturer at the medical school' in Hull, although the *Stamford Mercury* modified this to 'former lecturer'. In the opinion of the acknowledged arbiter on the question of the presence of arsenic in the stomach of Edward Bell, death had indisputably been caused by the poison. He had examined the stomach and had observed 'several small particles or patches like flour'. He had tested one of them, which had proved to be arsenic. The quantity of arsenic, in his opinion, had been sufficient to cause death.

It was a surprisingly brief account by the expert and was even more brief as reported by the *Stamford Mercury*. However, weight of medical opinion was consistent in its conclusions, and a means of murder was established.

Horace Watson, the next witness, was in many respects the most important. He had already appeared at the inquest to confirm that Mrs Bell had purchased a quantity of arsenic from his shop on the day before her husband had died. The Laceby chemist was able to tell the judge and the jury a good deal more about Jane Bell; at the same time, he also told them a good deal more about Horace Watson.

Mr Watson was clearly a man of great energy, enterprise and business acumen. In 1856, he was described in White's *Directory* as a grocer, corn miller, printer, chemist and druggist. In addition, he was the proprietor of *Watson's Pills*, more specifically of *Watson's Family Pills*, a patent medicine which enjoyed great success in the county.

Commercially available since around 1838 and still being sold in 1925, the pills claimed to be an efficacious cure 'especially for disorders of the stomach and digestive organs' which combined 'the mildest aperient with the finest tonic and aromatic preparations'. The purchaser of *Watson's Family Pills* was assured that the product was 'totally free from any mineral or drastic purge'.

Perhaps buoyed by commercial success, as well as by a number of dubious testimonials from the Louth and Horncastle areas, an advertisement of 1855 published in the *Stamford Mercury* claimed that 'the sale of these pills in Lincolnshire is greater than any other patent medicine'. Not only did the sales increase, but so did the number of conditions which the pills could cure. An advert in the *Louth and North Lincolnshire Advertiser* published in 1859, for example, listed colic, jaundice, piles, asthma, sore throat, erysipelas, scurvy, scorbutic eruptions and sore legs, amongst the conditions recommended for treatment by the pills. The rhetoric, constructed around superficial medical language was persuasive: *Watson's Family Pills*, it was claimed, 'remove all oppressive accumulations, regulate the secretion of the liver, strengthen the stomach, purify the blood, cleanse the skin of blotches, pimples or sallowness'.

Whilst Mr Watson's promotion of his product was robust and confident, he was occasionally careful enough and modest enough, not to exaggerate the virtues of the pills, warning the reader that, 'The Proprietor does not bring them before the public as a medicine for every disease'.

Horace Watson remembered the visit of Jane Bell to buy arsenic in some detail. She had asked for 'some of the stuff' which she had purchased the year before to kill bugs: the preparation was composed of arsenic and soft soap. She also asked to loan the same iron pot which she had used when she had bought the mixture previously.

He had told her to come back later, at about 7 or 8 o'clock, which she did, but he had not had the time to retrieve the pot nor prepare the mixture. Mr Watson suggested that she return in the morning, but Mrs Bell was insistent that she should have the mixture that evening, as her sister was coming to see her and she would assist her in using it to kill the bugs. Mr Watson relented and his assistant, who later turned out to be his brother, Octavius Watson, weighed her four ounces of arsenic and four ounces of soap. Horace Watson, not surprisingly, made it clear that the word 'poison' had prudently been written on the outside of the paper in which the arsenic was wrapped.

The narrative, as reported in the *Lincolnshire*

Chronicle, or as spoken by Horace Watson, seemed to get temporarily diverted, as it was revealed that a woman by the name of Eliza Burton had visited his shop the day before Mrs Bell and had tried to buy arsenic, but he had refused to sell her any. The second piece of apparently random information was that Horace Watson had some time ago assisted in pumping the stomach of Edward Bell, after he had taken a quantity of opium. The relevance of both incidents would only become clear as the case progressed.

Horace Watson continued his evidence by revealing that on hearing about the death of Edward Bell, the day after Mrs Bell had bought arsenic from him, he had immediately gone round to the house. She told him that her husband was not dead and that he had come round again; the strange second part of the statement may well be a piece of misreporting: the version in the *Stamford Mercury* recorded Mrs Bell having said, 'he had not quite gone and would revive again', which seemed less improbable than the version published in the *Lincolnshire Chronicle*.

In what might be seen as a breathtakingly tactless intrusion into the life of woman whose husband was either dead or on the point of death, the Laceby chemist marched up her stairs and started asking the niece of Mrs Bell questions concerning the death of her uncle. The amateur sleuth confided to the court that he suspected Mrs Bell had overheard the conversation, as when he returned downstairs, she told him, rather defensively, that she had placed the arsenic which she had bought from him in a safe place 'just as he gave it to her'.

Obviously dissatisfied with the outcome of his first visit, Horace Watson later returned, accompanied by Mr Leppington, and was of the opinion that 'for the satisfaction and peace of mind' of Mrs Bell, it was necessary that some enquiries should be made. The pompous hollowness of Watson's declaration perhaps suggests more of a concern for the satisfaction and peace of mind of a chemist with a commercial reputation to protect than for Jane Bell's well-being.

It seems clear that Mrs Bell was once again pressed on the subject of the arsenic, as she told Watson that she had added it to the chamber lye and placed it 'in the back place'. With the air of a man on the trail of the undeniable truth, the witness told the court, rather darkly, that 'the prisoner did not produce it'.

Having presumptuously initiated a one man investigation into a suspicious death in the village, Horace Watson returned the next morning and asked Mrs Bell to produce the arsenic, to which she replied that her mother had thrown it on the manure heap.

Just in case the judge and jury had not picked up the clues of the circumstantial, Mr Watson recalled further information which was presented as suspicious. Sometime before the death of her husband, Mrs Bell had bought some oxalic acid from his wife, claiming that the poisonous substance was to clean her husband's boots. The eagle-eyed Watson had noticed that Mr Bell's boots were still dirty and required an explanation from her: the reason why she had not got round to cleaning them was simply that her husband had been taken ill.

Jane Bell had also recently bought some tartaric acid and carbonate of soda from his shop, which she claimed were needed to prevent her husband being sick. Horace Watson, however, had taken the opportunity to snoop round Mrs Bell's house and had found the paper containing the tartaric acid, discovering that only a small part of it had been administered. In addition, he had also found oxalic acid in a paper, but it was not the same paper package which had been sold to her. The witness told the court that he would certainly have recognised the packet if it had been the one sold to Mrs Bell, as it had the word 'poison' written on it 'in a very peculiar manner'.

It is difficult to understand the relevance of the stories of oxalic acid, tartaric acid and carbonate of soda other than as a farrago of spurious evidence intended to create an impression of Mrs Bell as a guilty woman and of Horace Watson as a man of some consequence.

According to the *Evening Mail*, a London

newspaper which covered the trial in some detail, on hearing the chemist's testimony, an incensed Mrs Bell had exclaimed to the court that 'Mr Watson had never questioned her with regard to the arsenic and oxalic acid'. It was an informal intervention which was not appreciated by his Lordship, who advised the prisoner that she would have the opportunity to speak in due course, but at present 'she had better confine herself to the asking of questions, if she had any to ask'. It was a reasonable point of order, but a somewhat unrealistic one in view of Mrs Bell's unfamiliarity with such formal procedures as well as her probable lack of competence to frame such questions effectively.

In contrast to the lengthy deposition of his brother, Octavius Watson, was brief and to the point. He confirmed who he was and corroborated the sale of the arsenic.

The appearance of Eliza Burton, the wife of Thomas Burton, an agricultural labourer, resident in Laceby, presented interesting evidence relating to the purchase of arsenic and, at the same time, clarified the significance of the reference to her by Horace Watson in his deposition.

Mrs Burton had been at the house on the 24th March and according to her was asked by Mrs Bell if she would go and purchase a pennyworth of arsenic from Horace Watson in order to kill mice. The reason for making the request was that Mr Watson would probably refuse to sell her it, as he knew that her husband had taken poison in the past. The excuse seemed to confirm the story that Horace Watson had assisted in removing opium from Edward Bell's stomach. The *Stamford Mercury* provided the additional information that Eliza Burton went the shop and was refused, went a second time, and was refused again. If true, it demonstrated either the persistence of Mrs Burton or the solid principles of Mr Watson when selling dangerous chemicals.

Mrs Burton confirmed that she had seen Edward Bell at the house between 8 and 9 o'clock and that he was in great pain; she also confirmed that she had been in the house 'at the time Mr Watson was making his enquiries', although she did not make clear which of the three fact-finding missions conducted by the Laceby chemist she meant.

The final part of her deposition added further information concerning the request to buy arsenic. She had asked Mrs Bell why she needed poison when only the day before her daughter had bought some in Grimsby; to which Mrs Bell replied that her daughter had lost it on the way home. The story of a young girl of around twelve years of age being sent on a nine mile round trip to purchase arsenic in Grimsby seemed even less probable than her losing it on the way back.

After the death of her husband, Mrs Burton accompanied Jane Bell to see Mr Leppington. During the course of the journey, Mrs Bell had started a conversation about a woman in Immingham who had poisoned her husband, declaring that she could not imagine what she had been thinking to do such a thing.

Faith Gibbons, the teenage niece of Jane Bell, had been at the house the night before her uncle had died and was probably the source of new evidence uncovered and presented to the resumed inquest. She deposed that her aunt had prepared some arrowroot for her uncle at 9 o'clock and had then taken it upstairs for him. He had commented that the preparation was 'very nasty' and shortly after began to retch, but was unable to bring anything up. At around midnight, her uncle complained of being in great pain, at which point he asked for more arrowroot; he was given three or four spoonsful by her aunt. The witness was unable to recall her uncle saying anything more, although he did retch once again after taking the arrowroot.

What followed, as reported by the *Lincolnshire Chronicle*, was an impressionistic pile up of loosely related recollections, probably made in response to questions from the Counsel for the Prosecution.

Edward Bell complained of being thirsty all night and Faith Gibbons had given him water. She did not know what had become of the remaining arrowroot preparation; her uncle did not have any medicine during the night. She recollected going downstairs in the night to pick up a hot bran poultice which had been prepared by Mrs Bell's daughters.

In the morning, Mrs Bell had brought some gruel upstairs, 'observing that it would not be half-bad taking' and gave her niece a taste of it. The gruel was given to Edward Bell who was immediately sick and continued to deteriorate, until he died at 9 o'clock that morning. She had no idea what became of the remainder of the gruel.

It was an interesting account of the treatment of a desperately ill man with inadequate means, but seemed to offer little hard fact beyond the circumstantial evidence of Mrs Bell providing the most basic food and administering a traditional remedy for stomach and intestinal disorders, probably less expensive than *Watson's Family Pills*.

Robert Willson, the parish constable and village blacksmith, provided little beyond a strong argument for the professionalisation of the police: having been instructed by the magistrates to examine the beds and bedsteads of Mrs Bell, he had failed to find any evidence of bugs, 'nor even the appearance of one'.

What was of greater interest than the investigative failures of Robert Willson, was his recollection of the words voiced by Mrs Bell when he apprehended her. She repeated a version of the words spoken in her own defence in front of the magistrates concerning her innocence; in addition, she also referred disparagingly to Horace Watson, saying 'that cursed Watson would betray her and she had nothing to do but prepare to die'. The *Stamford Mercury* gave a different version of Mrs Bell's words, however, which did not include a reference to Horace Watson: 'Curse the stuff; I wish that I had not thrown it away'. It may have been just a coincidence that Mr Watson was a regular advertiser in the newspaper.

Both the *Lincolnshire Chronicle* and the *Stamford Mercury* reported Mrs Bell's self-defence in some detail, but do not always duplicate each other. To some extent the differences between the two may be attributed to different reporting styles. In the version published by the *Lincolnshire Chronicle,* there is a strong sense that the reporter had imposed order on the material, in the interests of clarity and cohesion. In the version found in the *Stamford Mercury*, which described Mrs Bell's statement as 'long and rambling', there is more a sense of trying to recreate a sense of an authentic voice, rather than a neatly packaged piece of journalism.

The disparaging description of Jane Bell's statement in her own defence, requiring clarity of thinking and coherent marshalling of the arguments beyond her natural powers, was probably accurate. What its lack of sympathy did not take into account, however, was that she had spent the previous one hundred and seven days in Lincoln gaol, enduring a very difficult pregnancy, and sometimes, some very unsatisfactory medical attention.

As early as the 9th April, the second day of her incarceration, she was complaining of pains and spasms in her stomach, as well as having 'thrown up a little foul and bitter fluid'. Ralph Howett, the prison Surgeon, prescribed 'a quietening draught' to see her through the night and 'an opening mixture' for the following morning.

During the following morning, Mrs Bell was still complaining of 'uneasiness' in her stomach, but refused to take the medicine to open her bowels. Dr Howett's solution was the taking of 'some pills' and to consume nothing but water and tea. To some extent, this may have worked, in that on the 11th April, Mrs Bell was slightly better, although she still complained of stomach pains. The cautious optimism of the Surgeon was tempered, however, by him noting in his *Journal* that he feared a miscarriage. The next day she was happily free from pain, but was still 'weak and faint'.

The crisis in Mrs Bell's pregnancy seemed to have been averted, but on the 24th April, her health took a turn for the worse. She complained of pains in her back and in her stomach, which were accompanied by 'some vaginal discharge forming altogether and threatening a miscarriage'. Dr Howett was clearly alarmed, prescribing 'an anodyne draught' and ordering complete bed rest, as well as taking in only cold tea, gruel and barley water. His concern was evident in that he saw Mrs Bell again, at 8.30 that night, to check on her progress. She was free from abdominal pain, but still had discomfort in her back; there had also been less vaginal discharge. Unfortunately, Mrs Bell was now suffering from nausea and vomiting, and required further medication to see her through the night.

Visting her at 8.00, the following night, Dr Howett reported that Mrs Bell had enjoyed a quiet day, despite the occasional pains in her back and further vaginal discharges. Building upon this, he ordered a 'quietening draught' and a 'sedation mixture'. The strict dietary regime continued, but with barley water being replaced by sago.

The entry in his *Journal* for the next day, the 27th April, was a curious mixture of optimism and cynical scepticism. Mrs Bell was now suffering less pain throughout the night, was free from vaginal discharges and her bowels 'more moved'. On the other hand, 'ever since she came into the Castle' Dr Howett had suspected that she had been taking 'means to produce an abortion', adding, 'I still believe this to be the case'.

The satisfactory progress of Jane Bell's health

continued until the morning of the 16th May when, after a disturbed night, she suffered 'a violent attack of spasmodic pain in very short intervals'. These were confined to a 'a small space in the biliary duct, as if from the passage of a gall stone'.

After treatment to relieve the symptoms, the patient gradually became more comfortable, having 'a perfect pulse of 65, a natural colour and looking very well'. He also recorded that she had eaten some mutton for breakfast which 'possibly did not agree with her'.

By 8.00 at night, her back pain was less severe and there had been no haemorrhaging or discharge; however, she did complain of her 'old pain in the stomach'. The Surgeon ordered another quietening draught as well as an 'antispasmodic mixture' to see Mrs Bell through the night.

The reports on Jane Bell during the following four weeks are less frequent and less alarming, consisting mainly of occasional nausea, vomiting and slight stomach pains, one of which was diagnosed as indigestion attributed to 'potatoes she improperly ate'.

The most interesting entry refers to another prisoner, Elizabeth Jessop, who was reported as being 'much more calm and happier since she attended to Jane Bell's indisposition'. To her credit, she had shown 'considerable interest and great kindness' towards Mrs Bell. Elizabeth Jessop had been tried for murder on the same Calendar as Eliza Joyce in 1843, but had been acquitted on the grounds of insanity and had spent time in the Hull Refuge Asylum.

Surprisingly, the entries in Howett's *Journal*, recording the health problems of Jane Bell, end on the 17th June, just over four weeks before her trial. The attentiveness of Dr Howett, despite his unease about her behaviours, contrast with the recorded lack of attention to her spiritual progress from Henry Richter, the Chaplain, whose only contact seems to have been advising her on entry to Lincoln gaol and his only concern a single absence from chapel, as she had been unwell.

The version of Mrs Bell's statement in the *Lincolnshire Chronicle* is a clear exposition of the life of woman having to deal with a feckless husband. Edward Bell 'had been in the habit of working in Hull' and she had been in the habit of going there every fortnight to collect his wages – perhaps a pre-emptive strike to prevent him spending it. A short time before his death, he had returned home very ill. He had suffered poor health for three years, or 'at least since he had taken poison'.

In response to his most recent illness, Mrs Bell had gone to see the Relieving Officers, who had sent Mr Leppington to attend him. His illness continued and Mr Leppington therefore continued to attend him. Mrs Bell had carefully administered the medicine ordered for her husband by the doctor. During his illness, he continually complained of thirst; Mrs Bell also described her husband as being 'off his head'.

Up to the morning on which her husband had died, she had not been able to change her clothes for five days, as she had to sit up with him. Before he died, Edward Bell had told his wife that he thought he was going to die, struggled out of bed with her assistance and kissed her: he died fifteen minutes later.

According to the newspaper report, Mrs Bell burst into tears at this point in her statement.

She ended her defence by recounting that her husband had taken opium three years ago when she was confined in bed. She had discovered it and had immediately sought medical advice; her husband's life had been saved, but he had never been well since.

Mrs Bell had bought a bedstead which had bugs in it and that was the reason why she wanted arsenic and soap from Mr Watson.

The report in the *Stamford Mercury* began by describing the accused as appearing to be suffering greatly as she spoke, which after one hundred and seven days in Lincoln gaol should perhaps have come as no surprise. The description of the statement as 'rambling' was confirmed by her opening words which obscured the chronology of a husband working in Yorkshire and him returning home ill. Sudden topic switches also made a contribution to the confusion, as her narrative moved rapidly from her husband being ill, to being persuaded to eat a little gruel which made him 'violently sick for a week'. When explaining straightforward incidents, as reported in the *Lincolnshire Chronicle*, the statement often became cluttered with superfluous details, such as Mr Leppington not having attended her husband until the Thursday, her husband having spent four pence on opium and that she had paid six shillings less than the asking price of the bedstead on account of the infestation of bugs.

The report certainly created a sense of the spontaneous speaking voice, but sometimes at the expense of the reader's ease of understanding. At the same time, it perhaps gave weight to the dismissive observation of the *Nottingham Review and General Advertiser for the Midland Counties* newspaper of the 25th July, and repeated in other publications, that Mrs Bell was 'a woman of the lower ranks of life'.

The reported final utterance, however, was clear enough: during the previous summer, her husband gave up work 'and lay in bed all the time'. What was not clear, however, was whether the root cause of Mr Bell's indisposition was illness, or opium, or both.

Both newspapers agreed that Justice Mawle, in his summing up, thought that little or no evidence had been presented to the court which linked Mrs Bell to the death of her husband through arsenic poisoning. Recalling his words at the opening of the session, his Lordship directed the Grand Jury to acquit the prisoner, should they entertain any doubts about her guilt.

Unfortunately, the exact details of those doubts which Justice Mawle would have expounded to the court, were not reported, apart from the *Stamford Mercury* mentioning that his Lordship had explained the frequent exclamations of innocence by Mrs Bell as being quite natural coming from 'a person concerning whom certain reports had been circulating'.

Other fragments of the summing up were made available by various newspapers beyond the county, which supplement our understanding of his Lordship's view of the case. In broad terms, he thought the circumstantial evidence 'was not so full and complete as was desirable', according to the *Evening Mail*.

Despite its astonishing overuse of distracting ellipses in its report on the case, the *Hull Advertiser and Exchange Gazette*, was helpful in recording some of the specific doubts voiced by Justice Mawle. He had 'dwelt minutely' on the absence of concealment by Mrs Bell in her procurement of the arsenic and had strongly suggested that Edward Bell was as likely to have poisoned himself as his wife, or any other person in the house at the time.

His Lordship also expressed very serious doubts about the alleged words of Mrs Bell to the parish constable.

That Robert Willson was a source of some amusement to his Lordship, as well as of considerable scepticism, was confirmed by the *Stamford Mercury*: with his tongue firmly planted in his judicial cheek, Justice Mawle helpfully made a wry observation on the parish constable's detective work: 'As to there being no bugs in the bed, bugs <do> not ostentatiously come forth to exhibit themselves to constables; but those who slept on the bed might fear their bite'.

The Grand Jury, whose members included one of the magistrates who had sent Mrs Bell for trial in Lincoln, followed his Lordship's advice and direction: after seventeen minutes of deliberation Mrs Bell was acquitted.

Appendix

Key Players In The Story Of Jane Bell

ALLIX, Charles. Served on Grand Jury at the trial of Jane Bell, at Lincoln Assizes. Resident of West Willoughby Hall.

ANDERSON, Sir Charles Henry John. Served on Grand Jury at the trial of Jane Bell, at Lincoln Assizes. Resident of Lea Hall.

BELL, Edward. Higgler, resident of Laceby. Died 26th March, 1845 of arsenic poisoning.

BELL, Jane. Tried for the wilful murder of her husband at Lincoln Assizes. Acquitted by Grand Jury.

BELL, John. Surgeon and apothecary. Conducted post mortem on body of Edward Bell. Gave evidence at the trial of Jane Bell, at Lincoln Assizes. Resident of Victoria Street, Grimsby.

BOUCHERETT, Ayscough. Served on Grand Jury at the trial of Jane Bell, at Lincoln Assizes. Resident of Willingham House, North Willingham.

BURTON, Eliza. Wife of Thomas Burton, agricultural labourer. Gave evidence at the trial of Jane Bell, at Lincoln Assizes. Resident of Laceby.

BROMHEAD, John. Served on Grand Jury at the trial of Jane Bell, at Lincoln Assizes. Resident of The Close, Lincoln.

BROWN, Francis. Served on Grand Jury at the trial of Jane Bell, at Lincoln Assizes. Resident of Welbourne.

CHAPLIN, Charles. Served on Grand Jury at the trial of Jane Bell, at Lincoln Assizes. Resident of Blankney Hall.

CHAPLIN, Colonel Thomas. Served on Grand Jury at the trial of Jane Bell, at Lincoln Assizes.

CHRISTOPHER, Robert Adam. MP. Served on Grand Jury at the trial of Jane Bell, at Lincoln Assizes. Resident of Bloxholm Hall.

CORBETT, Thomas George. Served on Grand Jury at the trial of Jane Bell, at Lincoln Assizes. Resident of Elsham Hall.

CRACROFT, Robert. Served on Grand Jury at the trial of Jane Bell, at Lincoln Assizes. Resident of Hackthorn Hall.

FARDELL, John. Served on Grand Jury at the trial of Jane Bell, at Lincoln Assizes. Resident of Eastgate, Lincoln and Holbeck Lodge.

FFYTCHE, John Lewis. Served on Grand Jury at the trial of Jane Bell, at Lincoln Assizes. Resident of Thorpe Hall, South Elkington.

GEDGE, Reverend Joseph. Magistrate at hearing into the death of Edward Bell at Grimsby Magistrates' Court. Resident of Humberstone.

GIBBONS, Faith. Gave evidence at the trial of Jane Bell, at Lincoln Assizes.

HOWETT, Dr Ralph. Prison Surgeon of Lincoln Castle. Attended Jane Bell during her incarceration awaiting trial.

HUTTON, William. Served on Grand Jury at the trial of Jane Bell, at Lincoln Assizes. Resident of Gate Burton Hall.

JESSOP, Elizabeth. Prisoner at Lincoln Castle. Supported Jane Bell during her incarceration awaiting trial.

JOHNSON, Theophilus Fairfax. Served on Grand Jury at the trial of Jane Bell, at Lincoln Assizes. Resident of Holland House, High Street, Spalding.

KEETLEY, Thomas Bell. Surgeon. Assisted in post mortem on body of Edward Bell. Gave evidence at the trial of Jane Bell, at Lincoln Assizes. Resident of Victoria Street, Grimsby.

LEPPINGTON, Dr Hildyard Marshall. Surgeon.

Attended Edward Bell. Conducted post mortem on body of Edward Bell, and gave evidence at inquest, Magistrates' court and Lincoln Assizes. Resident of Victoria Street, Grimsby.

LUARD, Charles B. Served on Grand Jury at the trial of Jane Bell, at Lincoln Assizes. Resident of Blyborough Hall.

MAINWARING, Charles. Served on Grand Jury at the trial of Jane Bell, at Lincoln Assizes. Resident of Coleby Hall.

MARRIS, George. Coroner at inquest and resumed inquest into the death of Edward Bell, held at the Waterloo Inn, Laceby.

MAWLE, Right Honourable Sir William Henry. Presiding judge at the trial of Jane Bell, Lincoln Assizes.

PACKE, George Hussey. Served on Grand Jury at the trial of Jane Bell, at Lincoln Assizes. Resident of Caythorpe Hall.

PEARSALL, Thomas John. Former lecturer at Hull School of Medicine. Gave evidence at the trial of Jane Bell, at the Lincoln Assizes. Resident of Hull.

REEVE, John. Served on Grand Jury at the trial of Jane Bell, at Lincoln Assizes. Resident of Leadenham House.

RICHTER, Reverend Henry William. Chaplain. Advised Jane Bell, during her incarceration at Lincoln Castle, awaiting trial.

SIBTHORP, Gervaise Tottenham Waldo. Served on Grand Jury at the trial of Jane Bell, at Lincoln Assizes. Resident of Canwick Hall.

THORALD, Richard. Magistrate at hearing into the death of Edward Bell at Grimsby Magistrates' Court. Served on Grand Jury at the trial of Jane Bell, at Lincoln Assizes. Resident of Weelsby House.

WATSON, Horace. Druggist. Gave evidence at inquest, Magistrates' court and Lincoln Assizes. Resident of Laceby.

WATSON, Octavius. Brother of Horace Watson. Gave evidence at the trial of Jane Bell, at Lincoln Assizes. Resident of Laceby.

WILDMAN, Richard. Counsel for the Prosecution at the trial of Jane Bell, at the Lincoln Assizes.

WILLSON, Robert. Parish constable and blacksmith. Gave evidence at the trial of Jane Bell, at Lincoln Assizes. Resident of Laceby.

WORSELY, Right Honourable Lord, MP. Foreman of Jury at the trial of Jane Bell at Lincoln Assizes.

WRIGHT, E. Served on Grand Jury at the trial of Jane Bell, at Lincoln Assizes.

YORKE, John Whiting. Served on Grand Jury at the trial of Jane Bell, at Lincoln Assizes. Resident of Walmsgate.

Chapter Two

Elizabeth Dodds (1838-?)

Elizabeth Dodds: Timeline

13th March, 1856: marriage of Elizabeth Bothamley to John Dodds, at Friskney Parish Church.

15th July, 1860: John Dodds taken ill.

17th July, 1860: John Dodds attended by Dr Richard Cammack, treated for constipation of the bowel.

21st July, 1860: purchase of arsenic by Elizabeth Dodds from the shop of Henry Cherrington, in Leake.

22nd July, 1860: John Dodds attended by Dr Cammack, treated for English cholera.

: death of John Dodds, around 6 o'clock in the evening.

23rd July, 1860: burial of John Dodds.

2nd August, 1860: adjourned inquest into the death of John Dodds after exhumation of body, held at Angel Inn, Wrangle, before Coroner J C Little.

: Elizabeth Dodds arrested by Superintendent Manton and taken into custody in Boston, on suspicion of murder, to appear before Thomas Garfit at the Sessions House; remanded in custody at Skirbeck Quarter lock-up.

6th August, 1860: resumed inquest into death of John Dodds, at Angel Inn, Wrangle. Coroner's court jury finds Elizabeth Dodds guilty of murder of her husband and sent for trial at the Lincoln Assizes.

11th August, 1860: Elizabeth Dodds received into Lincoln Castle gaol.

17th November, 1860: trial date fixed.

7th December, 1860: trial of Elizabeth Dodds at Lincoln Assizes in front of the Honourable George William Wilshere, Baron Bramwell; found Not Guilty by a Grand Jury and acquitted.

'The Apple Tree Has Blossomed Twice This Year': The Acquittal Of Elizabeth Dodds

On the 4th August, 1860, the *Louth and North Lincolnshire Advertiser*, broke a story of suspected poisoning in the village of Wrangle, near Boston. The opening paragraph hooked the reader with a promise of 'rumours of a terrible nature' relating to the unexplained death of John Dodds, a labourer, who had died on the 23rd July. There had been an inquest into his death after the exhumation of the body and his wife was subsequently held in custody at the lock up in the Skirbeck Quarter, Boston.

The newspaper produced only a rapid summary report of the adjourned inquest, cautiously informing its readers that, 'Under the present circumstances of the case, it is not deemed advisable to make the whole of the facts known'.

However, despite its professed prudent approach, the report did favour the curious reader with a few alleged facts: it had been known for some time that John Dodds and his wife had been living 'on unfriendly terms' and that Mrs Dodds had 'frequently been heard to issue threats against her husband'. In addition, she had spoken to her neighbour about mourning, 'as if she was certain he would die'.

The *Lincolnshire Chronicle* of 10th August, published extended details of this latest sensational crime story in the Boston area, with the headline, 'Suspected Poisoning at Wrangle'. What followed would not have disappointed any of its readers, as the newspaper indulged itself in a familiar bout of sanctimonious soul-searching and finger wagging.

Lincolnshire's belief in itself as a beacon of civilisation and moral improvement had allegedly taken a serious dent: after having been able to congratulate itself for many years on having remained free from the blood and arsenic stains of murder, it was now compelled to lament that this was no longer the case.

The claim was vague in terms of a time-frame relating to cases of murder in the county, but well-informed readers were probably able to work that out for themselves. In the 1840's, there had been a number of high profile Lincolnshire murder trials, which were reported well beyond the county: William Lilburn of Lincoln (1842), Thomas Johnson of Croft (1843), Eliza Joyce of Boston (1844), Mary Ann Milner of Barnetby le Wold (1847) and John Ward of Lincoln (1849) had all been accused and found guilty of atrocious crimes, mainly against members of their own family.

In view of the absence of additional sensational murder trials until late into the 1850s, when Thomas Fuller Bacon of Stamford was accused of poisoning his mother in 1857, two years after allegedly committing the crime, and William Pickett and Henry Carey were hanged for the brutal killing of William Stevenson, near Sibsey, in 1859, the report seemed to be mourning the passing of a golden age, free from such moral outrages.

Even putting to one side the many unexplained deaths which never even got as far as a Coroner's court, either because of the drain on public finances or sheer indifference, such a claim of moral improvement was somewhat disingenuous. An examination of the number of attempted murders and violent deaths, reported by the newspaper itself, after which the perpetrator was either transported or did not have a true bill found against them through a lack of sufficient evidence, does little to confirm such cheery optimism concerning law and order in Lincolnshire during the 1850s.

If the reader required any further encouragement to read the story, it was provided by the description of the crime as 'the darkest in the list of any that disgrace the human race.' The hyperbole was justified by the additional information that a man had been poisoned by his wife, who rather than performing her sacred duty of loving, honouring and obeying him, had instead opted to send him unprepared 'to stand before the Tribunal of his Maker'.

Inquest On The Death Of John Dodds, Angel Inn, Wrangle, Thursday, 2nd August, 1860

The article went on to focus upon the inquest into the death of John Dodds, an agricultural labourer, held at the Angel Inn, Wrangle, on the 2nd August, before the Coroner and former Mayor of Boston, Mr J C Little. But by way of a further preamble, the reader was supplied with additional contextual information relating to the case, which was a mixture of scant fact, presumption, scandal and special pleading.

According to the reporter, John Dodds had been married for four years, but the relationship had been an unhappy one in which his wife had formed an adulterous relationship. On Saturday, 21st July, after John Dodds had been unwell for some days, his wife went to see the local doctor, Richard Cammack, to obtain medicine for him: she was given a tonic to take away by the doctor. On her way home, Mrs Dodds called at the shop of Mr Henry Cherrington, draper and grocer, in nearby Leake, and purchased a quarter of a pound of arsenic, allegedly as a cure for her husband's toothache.

During the course of the evening, John Dodds became worse, and had to be attended at home by Dr Cammack, but despite his best medical exertions on behalf of the patient, he died the following day. 'Having no other means of judging', the doctor treated John Dodds as having suffered from bilious diarrhoea, and issued the death certificate on that basis.

The laudatory account of Dr Cammack's medical interventions was succeeded by more sombre information. Shortly after the death of John Dodds, 'strange rumours were set afloat' which led to the police investigating the matter and the Coroner ordering the exhumation of the body.

It was a coherent narrative, but fell well short of being an accurate one.

The first witness to depose was Dr Cammack himself, who was a well-established general practitioner in nearby Benington, whose father had been a Royal Navy Surgeon and who had also been in general practice in the village.

The evidence of Dr Cammack appeared to be clear and precise in its account of his dealings with John Dodds, establishing a useful timeline of key events. Initially, he had attended John Dodds to deal with an unpleasant constipation of the bowels. Dr Cammack had provided him with medicine to give him some relief from his difficulties.

On Saturday, the 21st July, Mrs Dodds reported to the doctor that her husband was feeling much better and she was given some 'strengthening medicine' to take home for him. The following day, the doctor was informed that Mr Dodds had gone out and caught a cold; further, he was 'incessantly sick' and required additional medicine. At this point, the timeline is rather compressed and not entirely clear: Dr Cammack made the decision to visit the house on account of the 'singular change' and, on arrival, he discovered John Dodds 'in a complete state of collapse': he was feeble, pulseless and 'appeared in a sinking state'. Despite being very ill, John Dodds was conscious and able to answer questions, telling the doctor that had been purged and that he had been vomiting throughout the night. The doctor had asked to look at any ejected matter, but was told that it had been thrown away.

Examining John Dodds, he found him to be thin and emaciated, at which point, he diagnosed English cholera, and prescribed accordingly.

This was the last time that Dr Cammack saw him alive, learning of his death on the evening of Sunday, 22nd July. In his opinion, the death was 'very sudden indeed', but without performing a post mortem examination, he could not account for it in terms of other causes.

At this point in the proceedings, the Coroner directed Dr Cammack and Dr Adam Mercer Adam, a distinguished Boston physician, to carry out a post mortem on John Dodds immediately, in order to establish the cause of death.

Whilst the two medical men were examining the

corpse of John Dodds, further evidence, of a more anecdotal nature, was provided by Mrs Susan Crane, wife of Wrangle labourer, Joseph Crane, and William Horrey (misspelt Orrey), the seventeen year old shop apprentice of Henry Cherrington.

With her husband, Mrs Crane had been a lodger at the time of Mr Dodds' illness and subsequent death. She deposed that John Dodds was taken ill on Sunday, 15th July 'with a violent sickness' and that by Tuesday, 17th July, he was so ill that Mrs Dodds went to alert Dr Cammack, who came to see him. Mrs Crane seemed to have been observing matters closely, as she was able to tell the inquest that the deceased's bowels were 'in a confined state' and that he 'had no passage until Thursday', after which his health rapidly improved, until the Saturday evening: at around 6 o'clock, his condition appeared to deteriorate significantly. Mrs Dodds and Mrs Crane tried to help the sick man by way of brandy, which he could not keep down, and by bathing his body with medicated lotions, before sending for Dr Cammack.

According to Mrs Crane, John Dodds died just after 3 o'clock on the afternoon of Sunday, 22nd July.

In addition to the account of the illness, Mrs Crane confirmed that there had been no domestic disharmony between John Dodds and his wife, other than the occasional disagreement: 'I never heard any threat on either side'.

If the deposition of Mrs Crane appeared to remove the well-worn motif of marital difficulties from the judicial reckoning, the testimony of young William Horrey rapidly brought it back again.

On Saturday, 21st July, Mrs Dodds had visited the shop of Mr Cherrington, at Leake, and asked for a quarter of a pound of arsenic 'to cure her husband's toothache', which he readily supplied. At this point, the jury may well have taken a keen interest, although Mrs Dodds had clearly not done anything wrong in purchasing poison, albeit in such a large quantity. What followed from the apprentice grocer was a prejudicial description of a subsequent visit to the shop by Mrs Dodds after the death of her husband. The visit took place on the Friday after John Dodds had died, when she told Horrey the news of his death, but 'seemed to treat the matter very lightly'. On the afternoon of that day, Horrey had seen the same parcel of arsenic which he had sold to Mrs Dodds: it had been opened and an ounce of the arsenic had been removed. The day after, Mrs Dodds came into the shop again and told him that she was not aware that the packet had been opened and that if her husband had been poisoned 'it was a very shocking thing'.

At this point, the medical men were ready to resume their expert testimony, having conducted a post mortem on the exhumed corpse. Dr Cammack reported back to the court that he had opened the abdomen and all parts were in a high state of congestion. It was his opinion that John Dodds had ingested an irritant poison, but wished to conduct further investigations into the viscera and suspicious red patches on the bowels. This was supported by the Coroner who explained to the jury that without a chemical analysis of those body parts it was impossible to ascertain the presence of arsenic.

Dr Adam agreed with the comments of Dr Cammack and supported his suggestion of further analysis 'as the appearances are suspicious of poison having been administered'. He also proposed that the inquest should be adjourned to allow time for further investigation.

Before the court was adjourned, Police Sergeant George William Gilbert of the County Constabulary provided an overview of the progress of the investigation so far.

On Friday, 27th July, Sergeant Gilbert had interviewed Mrs Dodds at her home, concerning the death of her husband. The focus of the questioning had clearly been on the purchase of arsenic from the Leake grocer, as Mrs Dodds was quite insistent that she had bought the substance as a treatment for her husband's toothache. In addition, she said that she had handed over the package to John Dodds, who had placed it in the hovel and that it remained unopened.

According to Gilbert, Mrs Dodds took him to the hovel, reached to the top of a wall and handed the package over to him, assuring him that she had known her husband to apply a spoonful of arsenic at a time to his gums in order to alleviate the pain.

The police officer had been of the opinion that there was sufficient evidence to implicate Elizabeth Dodds in the murder of her husband and she was ordered into the custody of Superintendent Thomas Manton.

On the adjournment of the inquest, Elizabeth Dodds was brought before the magistrate, Thomas Garfit, at the Sessions House in Boston, and remanded in custody.

Resumed Inquest On The Death Of John Dodds, Monday, 6th August, 1860

According to the *Lincolnshire Chronicle*, at the resumption of the inquest at 4 o'clock, on the 6th August, there was a good deal of local excitement. In the graphic description of the reporter, news had 'oozed out' that further investigations of the exhumed body had revealed the presence of poison in the stomach and viscera.

Dr Adam reported back to the court that he and Dr Cammack had done a thorough analysis of the body over two days. His findings confirmed the rumours which had given rise to so much excitement: the stomach and major organs all showed irrefutable evidence of the administration of arsenic. Further, the quantity of arsenic discovered was a large one, sufficient to cause death. Dr Adam assured the court that 'the best processes known for the detection of arsenic' had been used and that 'by every test we discovered the effect of arsenic', although he did not specify which chemical tests he had used.

However, it sounded conclusive evidence as to the cause of death.

An alert juror, clearly aware of the possibility that John Dodds' use of arsenic for pain relief might have caused his death, asked Dr Adam if the poison could have been administered in small doses over time. The response to the question, as reported by the newspaper, was a curious one which consisted of an assurance that the medicine bottle in the Dodds' house had been examined and no arsenic had been found in it; further, he offered the opinion that symptoms produced by large doses of arsenic were often the same as those arising from English cholera, and so any doctor would be justified in issuing a medical certificate to that effect, unless he suspected foul play. It seemed less an answer to a probing question about the death of John Dodds than a defence of Dr Cammack's professional competence in relation to a problematic area of medical diagnosis and, by extension, medical jurisprudence.

Dr Cammack was recalled to give further evidence, which amounted to very little other than that he had done a chemical analysis of the body and concurred with Dr Adam that the real cause of death was arsenic poisoning, 'as the whole system was saturated with that deadly poison'.

The inquest continued with several local witnesses who were acquainted with Mr and Mrs Dodds.

In essence, the deposition of Sarah Blake (*alias* Laming), was a recollection of an extended conversation that she had when Mrs Dodds visited her house three weeks previously. Initially, the exchange between the two women, who were clearly well-acquainted, was on the subject of clothes. Sarah Blake complimented her friend on looking 'nice and tidy', as she was better dressed than usual. What started as a commonplace exchange of domestic pleasantries, however, soon turned into a rather strange conversation about death and mourning. After having looked at herself approvingly in the mirror, Mrs Dodds declared that she should now dress up as her husband was going to die and she would therefore 'want another sweetheart'. The odd conversation continued upstairs, when Mrs Dodds asked Sarah Blake if she might see her mourning clothes and if necessary borrow them when required. Clearly surprised by the request, Sarah Blake diplomatically hoped that she would not require mourning clothes any time soon. At which point, Mrs Dodds told her that her husband had been very ill and that she thought that he did not have long to live.

Sarah Blake's testimony ended with a shocking and lurid piece of village gossip: she had heard that that there had been some domestic disharmony between Mr and Mrs Dodds in the past concerning an improper relationship between John Dodds and the mother of his wife, and that all three had quarrelled over the matter.

The second local witness was Mrs Harriet Adams who had been at the house of Mrs Dodds on the 9th July, making a white muslin dress. In passing, Elizabeth Dodds had commented that what she was making would make a nice wedding dress. Mrs Adams tactfully replied that she hoped that neither of them would need a wedding dress. Mrs Dodds, however, was quite insistent that John Dodds was going to die 'for the apple trees are in full bloom again'.

On a previous occasion, when visiting the house, Elizabeth Dodds had told her that her husband was uncomfortable with her 'getting too thick with a certain party', and that in response, she had told him 'that if ever he got jealous in his head she would give him cause for it'.

The deposition of Mrs Adams finished with yet another fragment of conversation, when she had expressed the hope that Mrs Dodds was not guilty of her husband's death, to which she had replied that she was not, and that it was her husband who had told her to buy the arsenic.

The testimony of Robert Leachman, an agricultural labourer, who had worked with John Dodds, was a short one. It verified that he had seen Dodds rub mercury into his gums in order to ease toothache. He had only seen him do it once and it was only a small quantity of white powder.

Superintendent Manton confirmed that he had apprehended Elizabeth Dodds on Thursday 2nd August, 'in consequence of what had taken place before the jury'. In reply to Manton telling her that she was being arrested on suspicion of poisoning her husband, Mrs Dodds denied the charge. The following day, he had taken Mrs Dodds to appear in front of Mr Garfit, the magistrate, and had requested that she be put on remand. On leaving the Sessions House, in Boston, Mrs Dodds had told the superintendent that she was 'as innocent of the charge as you are'. She also told him that after she had bought the arsenic, she came home and handed it over 'directly' to her husband in the garden. The superintendent had then asked Mrs Dodds if her husband was in the garden when she got home.

Perhaps as a follow-up to Manton's rather glib question, Mrs Crane was recalled to the stand. She was absolutely clear that when Mrs Dodds came home John Dodds was in the house. She also added that the next day, during his illness, he was in great pain and that he had expressed the fear that he was dying and needed to see the doctor.

The reported summary of the Coroner was brief to the point of being perfunctory: there could be no doubt that John Dodds had died of arsenic poisoning and it was equally certain that he did not administer it himself, given that he had expressed the desire to live. He further instructed the jury that if they thought that Mrs Dodds had administered the poison, they must find her guilty 'regardless of the consequences'.

Undeterred by the dark reminder that the jury might be initiating a process which sent Mrs Dodds to the gallows, it deliberated for only a short time after the court had been cleared, finding her guilty of the wilful murder of her husband.

The Coroner committed Mrs Dodds to be tried at the next Assize Session in Lincoln.

To end the report, the newspaper provided the information that Mrs Dodds was twenty-two years of age and had two children, one four years old and the other fourteen months, which was correct in every respect.

The story of the alleged Wrangle poisoning case was also reported in a number of other Lincolnshire newspapers at the time: the *Stamford Mercury* of the

10th August, which ran an extensive piece on the same day as the *Lincolnshire Chronicle*; the *Sleaford Gazette* of the 11th August, which drew much of its material from the *Stamford Mercury* and the *Louth and North Lincolnshire Advertiser*, also published on the 11th August, which reported only on the resumed inquest, and also drew its report entirely from the *Stamford Mercury*. Inevitably, there is a good deal of duplication of information in the reports, often verbatim, but there are also some interesting additions and variants, which occasionally provide greater clarity, although sometimes muddy the waters.

Starting with the punchy headline 'Poisoning a Husband', the *Stamford Mercury* had a preamble which focused upon the impact of the murder on the local community, in contrast to the worthy reflections on moral improvement and civilisation found in the *Lincolnshire Chronicle*. Wrangle, for the last eight or nine days, it reported, had been thrown into 'great excitement and consternation' by the sudden and mysterious death of a labourer who had lived in the parish for many years.

Before reporting on the proceedings, the Stamford newspaper first provided an overview of the essential narrative strands of the case, which included material not mentioned by the *Lincolnshire Chronicle* and which seemed to fill in some of the gaps left by the Lincoln publication. Most notably, it provided more specific information relating to the reason for the exhumation of the body of John Dodds, beyond the vague reference to 'strange rumours' which had alerted the police and the Coroner.

According to the *Stamford Mercury*, William Horrey, the apprentice who sold the arsenic to Mrs Dodds, and also the shop owner, Henry Cherrington, both played a more significant role in bringing the death of John Dodds to the attention of the authorities than the *Lincolnshire Chronicle* had stated. Both newspapers had reported that Mrs Dodds returned to the shop and had broken the news of her husband's death to William Horrey. According to the *Lincolnshire Chronicle*, Horrey had testified that Mrs Dodds told him of the death of her husband, but seemed to treat it as a trivial matter. The version in the *Stamford Mercury*, however, presented a slightly different sequence of events and used different language to describe those events. In response to William Horrey's polite enquiry about her husband's health, she 'coolly replied that he was taken seriously ill immediately she got home with the arsenic and died the following day'.

Nothing more was reported in the Lincoln newspaper about William Horrey after Mrs Dodds had left the shop that day; however, his part in the unfolding drama continued, according to the *Stamford Mercury*. After the encounter with Mrs Dodds, he voiced his concern to his master, Henry Cherrington, who 'became suspicious that all was not right'. Adding a little more colour to the routine information, the report noted that from this point onwards the Dodds case 'became the engrossing theme of conversation throughout the whole neighbourhood'. In due course, the conversation was joined 'by respectable parties' who, on hearing that an ounce of the purchased arsenic could not be found and thinking that the explanations of Elizabeth Dodds were 'far from satisfactory', informed the Coroner. As a result, an immediate exhumation and inquest was ordered.

The *Stamford Mercury* also provided the reader with additional interesting material from the expert testimony of Dr Adam at the resumed inquest. Based on his close chemical analysis of the viscera of John Dodds, he was of the opinion that the arsenic must have been administered in one or two large doses: if it had been ingested over a long period of time, he would not have been able to detect so great a quantity of arsenic as he did. The testimony of Dr Adam seemed to be ruling out the possibility that John Dodds had slowly poisoned himself through reckless self-medication for toothache, an explanation which had been probed by a juror, but which had not been clearly answered, if the report in the *Lincolnshire Chronicle* was accurate.

The report on the testimonies of the local

witnesses, on the whole, duplicated those in the Lincoln newspaper, with a couple of additions from Harriet Adams, Susan Crane and Robert Leachman.

Harriet Adams recalled having a conversation with Mrs Dodds concerning the death of her husband, whilst making her a black bonnet, telling her what local people were saying about the matter. In all probability, this was the context of Mrs Dodds' assertion to Harriet Adams, noted in the *Lincolnshire Chronicle*, that she had nothing to do with the poisoning of her husband.

The version of the testimony of Susan Crane was expanded to include the information that Mrs Dodds had given her husband some medicine at 3 o'clock, by which she meant, on Saturday, 21st July, three hours before he became very ill.

The statement made by Robert Leachman found in the *Stamford Mercury* differed significantly to that found in the version found in the *Lincolnshire Chronicle* in that he was apparently aware that John Dodds regularly used arsenic to alleviate the pain of toothache, as opposed to him having only seen him use it on one occasion.

The *Sleaford Gazette*, on the whole, reproduced the report in the *Stamford Mercury*, although it is clear that it was also familiar with the version in the *Lincolnshire Standard* in that it made use of its account of William Horrey's description of Mrs Dodds as treating the death of her husband 'lightly' and omitted the section found in the Stamford newspaper relating to the concerns of Henry Cherrington and their aftermath.

It was to be two months between Mrs Dodds being committed for trial in Lincoln and the trial actually taking place. During that time, she had to contend with the pressures of having a fifteen month old child with her in the gaol, her own poor health and, it later turned out, another pregnancy.

She was received into Lincoln gaol at 8 o'clock, on the evening of the 11th August. The first entry in the *Journal* of Ralph Howett, the prison Surgeon, records his initial impression of Elizabeth Dodds as being 'weak and emaciated as most women are who over suckle their children'. He also noted that the infant was 'a fine child' and 'it was high time it was weaned'. The weaning of the child was to become a bone of contention over the next few weeks, as the doctor ordered Mrs Dodds to stop breast feeding and she completely ignored him.

It was an evolving issue, not only for the Surgeon, but also for the Matron, who was supporting Dr Howett, the Chaplain whose main concern seemed to be the absence of Elizabeth Dodds from Chapel and the Governor, whose numerous entries in his *Journal* seemed highly concerned about the subversion of rules and expectations.

Piecing together the various journal entries, it seems that some kind of informal compromise position was reached, whereby the child was provided with half a pint of additional milk and two ounces of bread on a daily basis from the 23th August onwards, increasing to an additional two pints of milk on the 30th August.

If the additional prison food as a replacement for its mother's milk was intended to improve the health of Mrs Dodds and secure the health of the infant, it did not quite work. The *Journal* entry of the Surgeon for the 6th September recorded that in a matter of weeks the child had gone from being a 'fine child' to one in 'poor health': the consolation for Dr Howett, was that now the child was weaned it could be 'safely removed to the Union Workhouse or elsewhere'. That the child was eventually removed to the Boston Union Workhouse is confirmed by the Matron in her *Journal* entry for the 27th September. The health of Elizabeth Dodds did not improve and eventually, on the 11th October, Dr Howett realised, after witnessing a severe bout of morning sickness, that she was pregnant.

The most interesting aspect of the solution to the problem of Elizabeth Dodds and her child was the sharing of child care with another prisoner. Eliza Parker, awaiting trial for infanticide, and also to be acquitted at the Assizes, was recorded in the Matron's *Journal* of the 29th August as 'taking care of the Dodds child', along with the mother. It seems a practical solution in terms of the health of Mrs Dodds, although sharing child care with an alleged infanticide perhaps generated a different kind of difficulty. In addition, the Governor had recorded in his *Journal* that Eliza Parker herself, on entry into the gaol on the 28th August, appeared to be 'in a very delicate state of health'.

It may be that the arrangement was also seen as a practical solution to the frequent absences of Mrs Dodds from Chapel: the entries in the Governor's *Journal* between the 30th August and the 20th September, record the alternate absences of Elizabeth Dodds and Eliza Parker, as they presumably shared child care responsibilities on a rota basis. It appeared to have worked, as only one other absence from Chapel was recorded, this time by the Reverend Henry Richter, on the 23rd October.

The trial date for Elizabeth Dodds, and also for Eliza Parker, was fixed on the 17th November.

Trial Of Elizabeth Dodds, Lincoln Assizes, Friday, 7th December, 1860

The trial of the Elizabeth Dodds was reported at length by the *Lincolnshire Chronicle* on the 14th December.

Opening the business of the court, the Honourable

George William Wilshere, Baron Bramwell, who was visiting Lincoln for the first time, said that he found it difficult to compare previous Calendars with the present one. However, in his opening remarks, after the swearing in of the Grand Jury, he highlighted the fact that amongst the nineteen prisoners, four were accused of murder.

Eliza Parker of Old Bolingbroke, who had supported Mrs Dodds in prison, and Sarah Ann Mould of Rippingale, were both accused of the all too familiar crime of infanticide, Thomas Richardson, an agricultural labourer from Wyberton, was accused of fatally shooting a policeman, whilst Elizabeth Dodds was accused of poisoning her husband. Both women accused of infanticide were eventually discharged, there being no true bill found against them, although Eliza Parker was subsequently found guilty of the lesser charge of concealing a birth and was given three months hard labour. Thomas Richardson was tried, found guilty and sentenced to death, only to be reprieved by the Home Secretary two days before he was due to hang, given a life sentence and later transported to Western Australia.

The case of Elizabeth Dodds, Number 3 on the Calendar, was briefly outlined by Bramwell. There was no doubt that her husband had died from the administration of poison and so the issue for the Grand Jury was one of who had administered the fatal dose. It was equally clear that the prisoner had bought the poison, claiming that it was to alleviate her husband's toothache, but they must decide if it was in realty purchased 'for a bad purpose'. He also added that there had been a suggestion that the poison had been taken in some other medicine, 'the deceased being ill of another complaint at the time'.

As with Thomas Richardson, the Grand Jury found a true bill against Elizabeth Dodds.

The composition of the Grand Jury was more than usually impressive in terms of both local and national influence, including three Members of Parliament and two former Members of Parliament:

- (Hon) Alexander Leslie Melville (Foreman)
- J Allenby Junior
- Samuel Allenby
- John Bromhead
- Thomas Chaplin
- Richard Bergne-Coupland
- Colonel Weston Cracroft-Amcotts
- Thomas John Dixon
- William Robert Emeris
- Richard Gleed
- George Knowles Jarvis
- Alexander Samuel Leslie Melville
- (Hon) William John Monson MP
- Rev G A Moore

- George Hussey Packe MP
- William Parker
- Reverend Wilkinson Affleck Peacock
- Lieutenant-Colonel John Reeve Junior
- John Hassard Short
- Gervais Tottenham Waldo-Sibthorp MP
- Anthony Willson

The Counsel for the Prosecution consisted of Mr O'Brien and Mr Wake, whilst the Counsel for the Defence was Mr James Fitzjames Stephen, the recently appointed Recorder of Newark, who went on to achieve national distinction both as author, lawyer and judge, most memorably in the sensational trial of Florence Maybrick in 1889, at the Liverpool Assizes, who was also accused of poisoning her husband.

The opening address by Mr O'Brien started with a rather curious reference to the relative ages of Mrs and Mrs Dodds: the prisoner was a young woman and her husband at the time of his death was several years older. As a matter of fact, this was true: Elizabeth Dodds was twenty-two years old and John Dodds was thirty-two; as a matter of relevance, it seemed a tenuous starting point: such age differences were not unusual in Lincolnshire agricultural communities.

If the Counsel's knowledge of patterns of rural life was questionable, his awareness of medical issues was even more so. It was clear that Mr O'Brien was intent on establishing the familiar idea, cited in many C19th poison trials, that the victim enjoyed robust good health at the time of being poisoned. The Counsel for the Prosecution admitted that John Dodds had been suffering from a painful constipation of the bowels, which required medical attention, but seemed to be suggesting that the condition was irrelevant to the concept of good health.

Having established, at least to his own satisfaction, that a man should be cautious about marrying a woman ten years his junior and that an extended period of constipation did not constitute ill-health, Mr O'Brien talked the jury through the events leading to the death of John Dodds.

On Sunday, 15th July, he had complained of sickness and on the following Tuesday, he was prescribed 'two powders' by Dr Cammack, which finally took effect on the Thursday. On the Saturday, John Dodds spent a good deal of the day outside, making a rabbit hutch, taking a break to return indoors to eat 'a hearty dinner of tea and boiled meat', before resuming work on the hutch. These facts would be proved by the deposition of Mrs Crane who lived with Mr and Mrs Dodds.

John Dodds came back into the house at around six o'clock and appeared to be very ill. He went to bed and so was only in the living room for a short time that night. At 9 o'clock, he took some medicine, which had been left on the window sill by the prisoner. During the course of the night, he was sick and purged: at this point, it was also mentioned by Mr O'Brien that Elizabeth Dodds had 'emptied the evacuations away'.

John Dodds died in great agony at 3 o'clock the next day, despite Dr Cammack having provided him with 'a tonic to correct the disturbed state of the bowels' on the Saturday evening. In the judgement of the doctor at the time, John Dodds 'had succumbed under a sharp attack of English cholera'.

The account presented to the court, not surprisingly, was highly selective in terms of the involvement of Elizabeth Dodds in the events. She had provided her husband with a meal and also with medicine, both of which, by implication, might have contained poison. She also had removed useful evidence from the house which a doctor would have examined to confirm any suspicion of foul-play. What he did not mention was that Elizabeth Dodds twice contacted Dr Cammack concerning her husband's ill-health in order to obtain medical assistance for him, and that the doctor lived several miles away in Benington.

However, the more sinister agency of Mrs Dodds had been reserved by Counsel for the second-half of his opening speech. Mr O'Brien drew attention to the fact that on Tuesday, 24th July, stories were circulating that Elizabeth Dodds had purchased a large quantity of arsenic on the previous Saturday, the day when John Dodds became very ill. The reminder by Mr O'Brien was on the one hand surprising, on the other, damaging to his credibility, should the jury have been following the story in the press.

The precise date for the start of local speculation about Mrs Dodds and her possible involvement in the death of her husband seems oddly exact: it is true that the *Stamford Mercury* had reported such gossip in the district after Henry Cherrington had become suspicious, but no more. Unfortunately for the Prosecution, the words used to describe the start of that speculation were a close version of the news report found in the *Lincolnshire Chronicle* of 10th August: 'dark rumours *began to be afloat*'. Unless the reporter had decided to put a not very subtle variant of his own newspaper's account into the mouth of the Learned Counsel, it appears that Mr O'Brien was relying on the *Lincolnshire Chronicle* for some of his facts.

Mrs Dodds had allegedly purchased arsenic as a remedy for her husband's toothache, but Mr O'Brien was confident that he could prove that John Dodds was not troubled by toothache at the time of his death. Further, and perhaps more telling, it had been discovered that an ounce of the arsenic purchased by Mrs Dodds had been removed from the package.

Mr O'Brien then drew attention to the shocking

evidence provided by the medical men: quoting Dr Cammack, he highlighted the fact that the body of John Dodds had been 'saturated with arsenic'. More precisely, that one hundred and fifty grains of the substance had been discovered adhering to the stomach: the amount of arsenic was indeed astonishing, compared, for example, to the thirty to fifty grains conjectured to be in the body of Richard Biggadike by Professor Alfred Swaine Taylor at the trial of Priscilla Biggadike in 1868, which he had considered 'a large amount'.

Having established the possession of arsenic and the opportunity to administer it, Mr O'Brien moved on to the essential element of motivation. Predictably, in light of the evidence presented before the magistrates, the motive for the murder of John Dodds could be found in 'jealousy and dissension between the parties'. This had been confirmed by the conversation between the prisoner and Mrs Blake concerning the prediction of Mrs Dodds that her husband would die and that she would have to look for a new sweetheart, according to Mr O'Brien.

The opening of the case for the Prosecution over, Mr O'Brien completed the formalities by asking the Grand Jury to consider the facts and to 'arrive at a righteous decision'.

The first witness to be called was Samuel Hoyles, who lived with his brother in Friskney, half a mile from the Dodds' house. On the surface, the appearance of Samuel Hoyles, did little to extend the court's understanding of what took place, beyond confirming the story of Elizabeth Dodds that her husband had been very ill and that she went to Benington to get medicine from Dr Cammack. Hoyles, aged around fifteen at the time, had kindly given Mrs Dodds a lift to Benington, as he was going to Frieston, a few miles further up the road. Mrs Dodds had told him on the journey that she was going to get her husband some medicine as he was 'very bad' and she thought that he was going to die. Under cross-examination, the youth repeated what Mrs Dodds had said to him, but with a minor variation of language, 'Prisoner said her husband was very bad *then*, and said she believed he should die'. It was a small difference, but one which the Defence counsel later exploited.

The point in calling Samuel Hoyles to the witness stand was probably less to do with medical matters than to establish a specific connection in the minds of the jury between Mrs Dodds and the Hoyles family. Samuel Hoyles drew particular attention to the fact that he lived with his brother, which was only partially true: if the 1861 Census is correct, he lived with his father, mother and several siblings at the time, one of whom, Benjamin Hoyles, aged around twenty-six, was to be later identified as the source of marital friction in the Dodds household.

The testimony of Mrs Crane, who was lodging with the Dodds family, provided the same information about the illness of John Dodds and his treatment by Dr Cammack, as she had presented in the Coroner's court. However, in front of the Assize court, her memory seemed to become much more clear and detailed about the events of Saturday, 21st July.

In her earlier deposition, she said that John Dodds became very ill around 6 o'clock on the Saturday evening and that both she and Mrs Dodds tried to alleviate his distress, before summoning Dr Cammack. It had been a brief statement which was about to be expanded and altered into a narrative which was useful to the Prosecution.

According to Mrs Crane, John Dodds spent the Saturday morning in the garden making a rabbit hutch, whilst Elizabeth Dodds went to Benington, around seven miles away, to get medicine for her husband. On returning home, at around 2 o'clock, she removed the medicine from her pocket and placed it on the window sill. A few minutes later, Mrs Dodds asked her husband to take his medicine, but he declined, preferring to eat his dinner of fried meat and a cup of tea first.

After having returned to the garden, Mrs Dodds poured some medicine into a tea cup and took it out into the garden for her husband to drink. A few minutes later, she returned to the house, but her husband remained in the garden until six o'clock, at which point he began to feel very ill and went to bed. At 9 o'clock, Mrs Crane's husband persuaded him to drink some tea and Mrs Crane gave him some medicine 'but out of the bottle': it would not have required a sharp legal mind to have drawn the conclusion that Mrs Crane was comparing the administration of medicine out of a bottle with that having been poured into a cup of tea. Perhaps for the benefit of the jury, and certainly to the benefit of Mr O'Brien, Mrs Crane was quite insistent that John Dodds was vomiting continually after coming in from the garden at 6 o'clock. Just in case the point had been missed, Mrs Crane recalled that John Dodds had told her that he had drunk a lot of cold tea. In addition, he had said in her hearing that his wife would not have gone out to Benington for medicine unless she had got a ride, to which Elizabeth Dodds had taken exception, telling him, 'I have done my duty to you, and I have a good mind to say that the next medicine you want you shall fetch it yourself'.

Mr and Mrs Dodds went to bed between 9 and 10 o'clock that evening and Mrs Crane did not see the deceased until 9 o'clock the following morning, when he was still vomiting and purging. Mr Crane went to alert the doctor and remained in Benington in order to bring back medicine. On arrival at the Dodds home, Dr Cammack had asked to examine the motions of the ailing patient, but was informed by Mrs Dodds that they had been 'teemed away'. John Dodds died soon after three o'clock that afternoon.

The remainder of Mrs Crane's deposition was something of a piling up of miscellaneous anecdotal information, most of it detrimental to Elizabeth Dodds. She had never heard John Dodds complain of toothache and shortly after the day of the funeral, she had told her husband that people were saying that John Dodds had been poisoned and that he was going to be exhumed after the discovery of arsenic in the house. Mrs Dodds had overheard the conversation and had said that she did not believe he had been poisoned and insisted that the packet of arsenic found in the house had not been opened.

Under cross-examination Mrs Crane further deposed that when the policeman came to the house on the Friday, Mrs Dodds told him that she had forgotten that there was arsenic there. She also said that the deceased had been ailing for some time before his death.

Unfortunately, the report does not identify who cross-examined Mrs Crane, but her responses suggest that the highlighting of Mrs Dodds not remembering the arsenic may well have been prompted by the Prosecuting Counsel, whilst the information concerning the long-term ailments were probably pressed by Mr Stephen for the Defence.

In many respects, the key witness for the Prosecution was the young apprentice, William Horrey, who sold Mrs Dodds the arsenic. He confirmed the sale, but with the additional information that he had carefully wrapped the poison and labelled it 'Mercury poison': it was a familiar reminder deposed in many poison trials that the dispensing shop had taken the utmost care to protect the public. The label in question was shown to William Horrey whilst on the witness stand, who confirmed that the handwriting was his.

William Horrey presented a stripped down version of his deposition in front of the Coroner, confirming that Mrs Dodds had revisited the shop on the Friday and told him of her husband's death. In addition, however, he gave her visit a purpose in that she had called to buy some grey flannel. On the same day, the policeman had brought the packet of arsenic to the shop, which he weighed and confirmed that the was only three ounces left in it. Mrs Dodds, he said, was back in the shop the following day, asking 'if the poison was all right' and asserting that she did not believe her husband had been poisoned, but if it was the case, it was a shocking thing; and she also added that she did not know the packet had been opened.

The deposition was close to his evidence given at the resumed inquest, as reported by the *Lincolnshire Chronicle*. The difference was that William Horrey, in this latest version, gave the impression that he was very uncomfortable about being involved in the whole unfortunate business. In response to the question about the poison from Mrs Dodds, he quickly replied that the packet was now in the hands of the policeman and Mr Plant: James Plant was the Parish Clerk of Leake, as well as the Relieving Officer and Registrar for the Benington District. Even more telling were his brisk farewell words to Mrs Dodds after her denying any knowledge of the packet of arsenic being open: 'I have nothing to do with it'.

A witness who had not testified at the inquest, Elizabeth Greenfield, who lived two miles from the Dodds family, was called to the stand. Her evidence was brief and was not really a great deal of help to the jury. She recalled walking past John Dodds at 4 o'clock on Saturday 21st July, whilst he was working in the garden and had enquired after his health: he had replied that he was much better than he had been.

Robert Leachman, who worked with John Dodds, repeated his evidence from the inquest concerning having once seen his workmate rub his gums with mercury. More crucially, at least from the point of view of the Defence, he now added that John Dodds had told him that he frequently used it, and that he kept the substance in a small tin box in his pocket.

The following two witnesses were Superintendent Thomas Manton and Sergeant George William Gilbert.

It was no surprise that Superintendent Manton reproduced his evidence from the resumed inquest, relating to his arrest of Mrs Dodds after the initial inquest had been halted.

The straightlaced pocket-book deposition of Superintendent Manton produced nothing new. In contrast, the deposition of his colleague, Sergeant Gilbert, provided a little more detail about his visit of the 27th July to the Dodds house and, at the same time, unwittingly provided material that the Counsel for the Defence was able to exploit in his closing speech.

The discussion between Sergeant Gilbert and Mrs Dodds concerning her purchase of arsenic for her husband's toothache and her insistence that she had not opened the packet were familiar territory from his appearance at the initial inquest. So too the information that Mrs Dodds had taken the police officer to the hovel where the packet of arsenic, minus its string, had been placed. The new piece of information which Sergeant Gilbert introduced was that the packet in the hovel was 'quite exposed to view'. Mr Stephen at once saw the significance of this casual remark and immediately cross-examined the policeman: from his response, it was clear that the Counsel for the Defence had asked the Sergeant if he had provided this piece of information at the Coroner's court, but he had been unable to remember.

It may have been a convenient lapse of memory, but it was certainly a potentially embarrassing one, as his deposition at the inquest would have been a matter of public record.

In his opening remarks to the jury, Mr O'Brien had confidently identified a motive for the murder of John Dodds, rooted in 'jealousy and dissension'. The evidence for his assertion, he suggested, had been heard in the deposition of Sarah Blake in front of the Coroner when she recollected Mrs Dodds musing that she needed to look for a new sweetheart, as she thought her husband would soon be dead. The story did not present Mrs Dodds in a particularly good light, it is true, but it hardly seemed definitive evidence of marital difficulties. It may be that Mr O'Brien had made a mistake in referring to the evidence of Mrs Blake in this context, confusing her with Mrs Adams, who had produced a similar story in front of the Coroner, but with additional material related to the marital difficulties of Mr and Mrs Dodds.

In front of the Grand Jury and Baron Bramwell, Mrs Blake did not disappoint, producing a well-rehearsed narrative of vanity and insensitivity. It would have been a straightforward story for the court to follow, except perhaps for the reported declaration by Mrs Dodds that she knew her husband's death was imminent because 'the apple tree has blossomed twice this year'. It certainly puzzled Mr Stephen, who appeared to ask for clarification from Mrs Blake as to what Mrs Dodds had meant. The witness replied that: 'Many people believe in our neighbourhood that when the apple tree blossoms twice in the year, it is a sign of death'.

Harriet Adams, who followed Mrs Blake, also reproduced her evidence from the inquest, which related to the comments made by Mrs Dodds about the muslin dress which she was making resembling a wedding dress. She also recalled the conversation about the anticipated death of John Dodds, although interestingly, and possibly in the light of the question from Mr Stephen to Sarah Blake, she included an explanation of the apple blossom story, but making it clear that it was a belief 'in that neighbourhood'. It seems that Mrs Adams wished to distance herself from such quaint and fanciful folk wisdom.

What Mrs Adams did not wish to distance herself from, however, was a scurrilous story about Elizabeth Dodds. Her evidence at the inquest mentioned in passing that the prisoner had confided to her that her husband had been unhappy about his wife getting a little too close 'to a certain party'. In the version presented at the Assize court, Mrs Adams revealed the identity of the 'certain party': he was none other than Benjamin Hoyles, the brother of Samuel Hoyles who had appeared earlier in the proceedings.

Unfortunately, Benjamin Hoyles had not been

called as a witness to confirm the truth of the story, which might have strengthened the case for the Prosecution; on the other hand, a denial of its truth would have badly weakened the construction of a story of 'jealousy and dissension', as clear evidence to support a motive for murder.

In terms of the confirmation of arsenic poisoning, Dr Cammack was very obviously a key Prosecution witness, as was his colleague, Dr Adam, after having examined the body of John Dodds.

The deposition of Dr Cammack was also useful to the jury from the point of view of understanding the extent to which John Dodds enjoyed good health prior to being allegedly poisoned by his wife. In his previous deposition at the Coroner's court, Dr Cammack had provided an account of his treatment of John Dodds from Tuesday, 17th July until his death of Sunday, 22nd July, although it did not always provide sufficient detail to form a conclusive picture.

On this occasion, Dr Cammack took the jury carefully through his attendance of John Dodds, day by day, and also provided details of the medicines which he used to treat him.

On Tuesday, 17th July, he had received an order from the Relieving Officer to attend John Dodds. He saw Mr Dodds at his home and found him to be suffering from a constipation of the bowels: as a result, he sent the patient an aperient medicine. On the following Thursday, Elizabeth Dodds came for more medicine, as what he had prescribed had not had the desired effect: in fact, according to Mrs Dodds, he was worse, and required some 'opening medicine'. Dr Cammack obliged by providing 'a mixture of a stronger character', instructing Mrs Dodds to let him know if there was no further improvement. Around noon the day after, Mrs Dodds once again visited Dr Cammack: the medicine had successfully purged her husband, and he was feeling 'a little better'. As a follow up treatment, Dr Cammack sent Dodds 'a half-pint bottle of tonic medicine to strengthen him'.

The final contact Dr Cammack had with Mr Dodds was on the Sunday, after being summoned by Mr Crane, who had come to tell him that 'John Dodds was very bad'. Dr Cammack set out to see him having ordered Crane to remain and await his return so that he could take back the necessary medicine. He had found John Dodds in a state of collapse and after questioning Mrs Dodds and Mrs Crane, arrived at the conclusion that it was a case of English cholera. He had asked to see any evacuations, but was told that they had been thrown away.

On returning home, he immediately handed over to Mr Crane 'some stimulating medicine, and an order for a bottle of wine to strengthen him'. Unfortunately, John Dodds died that afternoon.

Dr Cammack added, perhaps in response to

a question or prompting from Mr O'Brien, 'the deceased did not complain of toothache'.

In most respects, the details of the account from Dr Cammack, agreed with other witness statements relating to the ill-health of John Dodds prior to being poisoned. In terms of a comprehensive account of events, however, it was a pity that Dr Cammack made no mention of Saturday, 21st July, the day on which, according to Mrs Crane, Elizabeth Dodds went to get medicine for her husband, in alleged contentious circumstances, and the day on which the arsenic was purchased in Leake.

The deposition of Dr Adam, as expected, supported the conclusions of Dr Cammack about the cause of death. He also provided additional observations on the dental health of John Dodds, which was clearly an important issue in the case: he had decayed teeth, but an examination of his gums showed no sign of them having been rubbed with arsenic.

Interestingly, it was later reported by the *Lincolnshire Chronicle* that Mr O'Brien applied to Baron Bramwell for additional costs in the case of Elizabeth Dodds, which he had incurred for the medical evidence. Unfortunately, the Judge did not have the power to award any extra costs, only statutory ones. Counsel for the Prosecution had clearly invested heavily in the testimonies of the medical men in order to win his case.

After the evidence of the medical men had been heard, Mr Stephen addressed the Grand Jury on behalf of Mrs Dodds. According to the *Lincolnshire Chronicle*, it was a speech which was both 'powerful and eloquent', lasting one and a half hours. The key points of the Defence speech were that no adequate motive had been established by the Prosecution and that the entirety of the evidence presented in court failed to connect Mrs Dodds to the poisoning of her husband. By way of an explanation, Mr Stephen strongly suggested that the deceased may have taken the poison by accident or design

Without going into detail, the newspaper described the speech as being 'an affecting appeal to the sympathies of the jury on behalf of the unfortunate prisoner at the bar'.

After the summing up by Justice Bramwell, outlining the case and the choice of verdict available, the Grand Jury retired for a few minutes and concluded that Mrs Dodds was not guilty of the wilful murder of her husband.

An extensive report of the trial was also published by the *Stamford Mercury* on the same day as the *Lincolnshire Chronicle*, and is an invaluable supplement to it. It included the occasional additional material from some of the witness statements, as well as clearer information about some of the cross-examinations. More importantly, its report of the Defence Counsel's closing speech is meticulous and detailed to the point of reading like an exact transcription: the reporter working for the *Stamford Mercury* either had a good working knowledge of shorthand or had access to Mr Stephen's notes.

The report of the Counsel for the Prosecution's opening speech differs in a few respects to that found in the *Lincolnshire Chronicle*, especially in some of the key terms of reference which the jury had been asked to consider.

If the reporting is correct, Mr O'Brien began his speech with a factual error: by way of introduction, he told the court that Mrs and Mrs Dodds had two children and that they had been married for two years. Unfortunately for Mr O'Brien, John Dodds and Elizabeth Bothamley were married at Friskney Parish Church, on the 13th March, 1856.

The issue of the health of John Dodds was highlighted in the *Stamford Mercury* version of the speech, although using slightly different terms from that recorded in the *Lincolnshire Chronicle*. Mr O'Brien conceded that there had been a health issue in early July, but had described it sceptically as a 'supposed…constipation of the bowel'; in addition, John Dodds had become very thin as a result of 'a poverty of food', not illness.

The opening remarks of the Prosecution drew attention in some detail to the evidence of Samuel

Hoyles. The jury should bear in mind, he insisted, that on the day that her husband was 'better and at work', she had told the boy that 'her husband was very bad and she thought he would die'. Further, and in contradiction, she had also told Dr Cammack that her husband was feeling much better, when he supplied her with a tonic mixture.

The limitation of a reliance on the words of a fifteen year old boy to prove that Mrs Dodds was a scheming, cynical liar, was later to be exposed by Mr Stephen in his closing speech.

The narrative of the poisoning constructed by Mr O'Brien was a simple one in which on returning from buying arsenic in Leake, Mrs Dodds gave her husband his medicine in the garden, and within three hours he became very ill and had died the next day.

The report of the speech in the *Lincolnshire Chronicle* focused upon jealousy which had produced difficulties in the relationship between Mr and Mrs Dodds, and therefore supplied a motive for murder. The *Stamford Mercury* duplicated the Prosecution line, but with an odd addition. Mr O'Brien stated that he was aware of the identity of the man with whom Mrs Dodds had been suspected of having an improper relationship, but he refused to mention his name. If true, it was either a bizarrely discreet piece of witness protection or the ground was too uncertain to bring him before the court: either way, it mattered very little, as a witness later let the cat out of the bag during the course of the proceedings.

The testimony of Samuel Hoyles, as reported by the *Stamford Mercury*, varied very little, although there seemed to be some geographical confusion on the part of the reporter, who had him driving his wagon the wrong way, in the direction of Friskney rather than Frieston. A cross-examination revealed that Samuel Hoyles had spoken about the ride he had given to Mrs Dodds and the conversation with her to Superintendent Manton, about a week after the death of John Dodds. He swore that she had said her husband was very bad and she thought he would die.

The reporting of the evidence of Mrs Crane added very little to that in the *Lincolnshire Chronicle*, beyond the specific time of 8 o'clock for Mrs Dodds leaving for Benington on the Saturday morning to collect medicine, and that Sergeant Gilbert had asked her about John Dodds using arsenic to cure his toothache.

Under cross-examination, Mrs Crane repeated the claim made by Elizabeth Dodds that she had forgotten all about the arsenic until the visit of the policeman. More damning for Mrs Dodds was Mrs Crane insisting that after drinking tea handed to him by his wife as he returned from the garden, the condition of John Dodds appeared to worsen, 'Whatever the deceased took he was sick after it'.

The account of the testimony of William Horrey started inauspiciously with a comical typographical error which renamed the witness as William Horror. It did, however, provide additional material, some of which clarified the vagueness of the *Lincolnshire Chronicle*.

On her first return to the shop on the Friday, Mrs Dodds had come into the shop to buy some grey flannel, as reported by the Lincoln newspaper, but added that she had said that she had to be careful now, as her husband had died, and she would 'have to go on the parish'. It may be that her concern about the economic realities of losing her husband being foremost in her mind explain the seventeen year old William Horrey's observation at the inquest that she took the death of her husband 'lightly'.

The *Lincolnshire Chronicle*, reporting the account of the second return to the shop, noted William Horrey having told Mrs Dodds that he had nothing to do with it, when discussing the offending packet of arsenic. The report in the *Stamford Mercury* recorded the same words, but adding 'the policeman has taken it'. The addition is helpful in understanding more clearly the context of Horrey's words, but the same sense of discomfort and closing down the conversation remained.

The cross-examination of the apprentice, not surprisingly, suggested a similar nervousness in a potentially tricky situation. He very carefully described the following of correct procedures when selling the arsenic to Mrs Dodds: 'I made the entry of sale of it in her presence, on the day she purchased it, and she signed it'. Helpfully, he added that he had never sold any arsenic to John Dodds.

The deposition of Elizabeth Greenfield reported in the *Lincolnshire Chronicle* seemed remarkably unimportant; the same words were recorded in the *Stamford Mercury*, but it also noted that Baron Bramwell stopped her from speaking any further, when he declared her evidence as inadmissible.

The account of the depositions of Robert Leachman and Superintendent Manton offered nothing different to the reader. That of Sergeant Gilbert, however, was a different matter, providing further excerpts from the conversation which he had with Mrs Dodds at her house. The deposition reported in the *Lincolnshire Chronicle* made it clear that the policeman was interested mainly in the arsenic bought by Mrs Dodds and now stored in the house, an investigative theme which had been apparent since the sergeant gave evidence at the inquest. The *Lincolnshire Chronicle* report on the inquest recorded that Mrs Dodds had told Sergeant Gilbert that she had known her husband take as much as a spoonful of arsenic at a time to rub on his gums. The remark had followed on from her handing over the packet of arsenic which had been opened and the discovery that an ounce had been removed, thus creating the impression that her comment was a quick-thinking explanation for the missing arsenic. However, in the account of the same incident later deposed at the Assize court, as reported by the *Stamford Mercury*, her comment about her husband's use of arsenic took on a different meaning. According to the sergeant, on being handed the packet he had remarked that 'it was dangerous stuff', to which Mrs Dodds replied 'as dangerous as it is, it was her husband used it as much as a spoonful at a time to rub his gums'. In other words, it was a natural continuation of a conversation topic, rather than a sudden switching of the agenda to cover her tracks.

The report of the deposition in the *Stamford Mercury* gave an extended version of the cross-examination of the sergeant which produced a greater sense of discomfort than the shorter version in the *Lincolnshire Chronicle*. Sergeant Gilbert was pressed on the issue of whether or not he had mentioned the details of his conversation at the inquest, which he could not remember. This was followed by additional material which gave the impression of a man attempting to restore some kind of professional credibility: he had searched the deceased's clothes for spoons, but failed to find any; what he did find were two small boxes, but neither of them showed any traces of arsenic in them.

The reporting of the depositions of Sarah Blake and Harriet Adams did not include anything left out by the *Lincoln Chronicle*, although interestingly, Mrs Adams' evidence about Benjamin Hoyles was not mentioned.

The evidence for the Prosecution ended with the testimony of Dr Cammack and Dr Adam, as reported in the *Lincolnshire Chronicle*, but also included some new material, including the questioning of the Benington doctor by the judge.

The report of the recollections by Dr Cammack of his treatment of John Dodds differed from that of the Lincoln newspaper in that after testifying that Elizabeth Dodds had told him that her husband was much better, she had added that now 'she did not require relief from the parish'. It was a detail, in its concern for domestic economics, which complemented her remarks to William Horrey on a similar theme. Dr Cammack also testified, as did many other witnesses, that he had never heard John Dodds complain about toothache.

Baron Bramwell was sufficiently interested in the chemistry of arsenic and its effect on the human body, as well as the behaviour of the substance when added to another liquid, to cross-examine Dr Cammack himself.

In response to the questions of the judge, Dr Cammack provided answers, but which did not always seem especially helpful. Arsenic, he said, would show its effects on the human body in one hour, in six hours, in twenty-four hours or forty-eight hours, depending upon the quantity of arsenic used and the amount of food in the stomach. The point was reasonable and obvious, but was not developed with any clarity by Dr Cammack when he followed it up. He told the judge and jury that the quantity of arsenic he had discovered in the body of John Dodds might have caused death in six, twenty-four or forty-eight hours: in the minds of the jury, such wide variation might have produced a sense that medical jurisprudence was not yet an exact science, at least in Benington.

The questioning by Justice Bramwell concerning the behaviour of arsenic in a liquid solution was clearly intended to throw some light on the Prosecution suggestion that Elizabeth Dodds had the opportunity to secretly add arsenic to the medicine prescribed by the doctor. Dr Cammack told the court that the medicine which he had sent for John Dodds would have been rather opaque if shaken up and that on account of its chemical structure, only a small amount of arsenic would dissolve in cold water. Based upon the quantity of arsenic found in the body, he doubted whether it would have remained in solution to have enabled the deceased to have drunk it all, unless he had continually stirred it, and failed to notice its grittiness in his mouth.

Dr Cammack had examined the gums of John Dodds, but was unable to say if arsenic had been applied. His final comment, presumably prompted by a precise question from the judge, was that people subject to constipation may also be subject to toothache: it was an odd piece of medical information.

Dr Adam's deposition, in its support of Dr Cammack, duplicated the report of the *Lincolnshire Chronicle*, although his comments upon the issue of detecting arsenic on the gums were reported slightly differently. In the opinion of Dr Adam, if John Dodds had rubbed his gums with arsenic and then swallowed it rapidly, it would not have produced an inflammation of the gums after death – which may have explained the inability of Dr Cammack to reach a definitive conclusion on the issue.

The Defence Counsel's closing speech, essentially a plea for the life of Elizabeth Dodds, was reported in remarkable detail: it was a skilful compound of clearly structured argument, feigned incredulity, lucid logic, barely concealed contempt for key witnesses and tough reasonableness.

He began by methodically dismantling the interpretations of ambiguous circumstantial evidence put forward by the Prosecution.

The key suspicious incidents highlighted by the Prosecution had been that Mrs Dodds had told a youth who had given her a lift that her husband was very ill, when he wasn't; and that she had added arsenic to her husband's medicine, as she walked past the place where it had been stored, between the house and the garden, and then gave it to him. 'If she did not poison him then she could not have poisoned him at all', he insisted.

As far as a motive was concerned, it had been based upon conversations 'with a couple of dressmakers' which involved flimsy remarks about her husband dying and mourning clothes. Further, the prisoner had thrown away the evacuations of her husband in an attempt to dispose of incriminating evidence.

According to Mr Stephen, this was the totality of the case against Mrs Dodds presented by the Prosecution. It was, of course, for the time being, a deliberately reduced account of the evidence against the defendant, omitting to mention the purchase of arsenic to provide the means of the crime and the stories of 'jealousy and dissension' as a motive.

Mr Stephen then moved from a general dissatisfaction with the case against Mrs Dodds to particular aspects which required the jury's close attention.

The conversation with Samuel Hoyles in which Mrs Dodds supposedly said that her husband was very ill should be treated with scepticism, he suggested, and declared that he did not think for one moment that the jury would believe the evidence of the youth.

Moving into a more rhetorical mode, the Counsel for the Defence asked whether it was credible that a woman who was planning a journey to buy arsenic to murder her husband would ask for a ride? The theatrical incredulity, tempered by a comparative grammatical analysis of the reported conversation, continued when Mr Stephen drew attention to the words which Samuel Hoyles swore he heard used by Mrs Dodds. In response to the enquiry about her husband's health, fifteen year old Samuel Hoyles had vigorously sworn, under cross-examination, that she had definitely said: 'He is very bad *then*'; Mr Stephen pointed out that this was clearly untrue, as she would have replied: 'He is very bad *now*'. The youth was 'so ignorant and inaccurate' that the only part of his evidence that could be believed was that he had given Mrs Dodds a ride to Benington. The calculated contempt for the accuracy of the memory of Samuel Hoyles, was only exceeded by his disdain for the reliability of a mere fifteen year old boy in a wagon from Friskney.

The key issue of the purchase of poison by Mrs Dodds for the sole purpose of murdering her husband, was addressed by the Defence Counsel with common sense logic. If she was buying arsenic for that purpose, as opposed to acting upon instructions from her husband, why would she make the purchase in Leake, where she was well-known, as opposed to

Benington seven miles away, where she was going anyway? Further, in known cases of arsenic poisoning it was invariable that poison was purchased under false pretences, most commonly for the destruction of vermin. On purchasing the arsenic, Mrs Dodds had explained that it was for the treatment of her husband's toothache, although he did concede it was an unlikely explanation: however, the Counsel for the Prosecution had himself called a witness, Robert Leachman, who confirmed that John Dodds had indeed used arsenic as a cure for toothache, improbable as that may seem.

The sequence of events allegedly leading to the administering of poisoned medicine was examined by Mr Stephen with the same cool logic. Mrs Crane had deposed that Elizabeth Dodds had pressed her husband to take his medicine before eating his dinner, but he had declined the offer: the Defence Counsel politely queried the idea of trying to carry out a murder in full view of a witness. Mrs Crane had also observed Elizabeth Dodds pouring the medicine into a cup and going into the garden with it to give her husband, passing by the hovel where the arsenic had been put for safe keeping. Prosecution had made the case for Mrs Dodds taking the opportunity to add arsenic to the cup on her way to the garden. In response, Mr Stephen once again referred to evidence which had emerged in court from a witness under cross-examination, namely Sergeant Gilbert when he visited the house. He reminded the jury that, according to the policeman, the packet of arsenic had been placed on open view and that Mrs Dodds consistently maintained that she did not know that it had been opened. In mock derision, Mr Stephen dismissed the concept of a woman killing her husband with arsenic who would leave the agent of his death visible for anyone to see, rather than disposing of the remaining poison. Further, it was totally unbelievable that she would persist in 'a foolish and stupid lie' which was so easily contradicted, unless she was telling the truth. In short, Mr Stephen was suggesting to the jury that if Elizabeth Dodds was a murderer, she was a ridiculously incompetent one. He was equally dismissive of the evidence of conversations suggesting that Mrs Dodds wanted to be rid of her husband, describing it as mere 'village gossip'.

The serious issue, he insisted, was how such a large quantity of arsenic could find its way into the body of John Dodds. The Defence Counsel was quite brutal in answering his own question: if a man was stupid enough to use such a dangerous substance to cure toothache, it was equally likely he was stupid enough to ingest a large quantity without thinking about the consequences and believing it would do him good. It had been established from Dr Cammack, under questioning from Baron Bramwell, that the heaviness of the arsenic meant that it could only be held in suspension by constant stirring, and in addition, it was a rough and gritty substance: on both counts, the husband would have noticed the presence of the arsenic in his medicine and it was therefore reasonable to assume that he had administered it himself.

But Mr Stephen was not done yet. He allowed the possibility that if John Dodds had had a serious quarrel with his wife, he might have taken the arsenic intentionally to poison himself, perhaps out of spite. There had been mention of jealousy by a single witness, but this had amounted to one sentence on one occasion; if there had been other occasions, Mrs Crane, who lived with the couple, would have known about them: so too would have the whole neighbourhood. Without overplaying his hand, but at the same time presenting himself to the jury as an impartial and reasonable man, Mr Stephen proffered two clear options for the jury to consider: either John Dodds had killed himself or his wife had murdered him: 'there was just as much reason for believing one or the other'. It was the reasonableness of a man who was confident of a decision in his and his client's favour; however, as an additional security, Mr Stephen anticipated the objection that John Dodds had no reason to commit suicide nor had shown any suicidal tendencies before his death. If this was the case, the Defence Counsel argued, he would not be the first man to take his own life 'without giving notice of his determination or state of mind'; and further to the point, having done so he would have cast suspicion on his wife and would be 'guilty of a great wrong'.

The summing up by Judge Bramwell, as reported, was even-handed and possibly reflected his own lack of certainty about the case. He suggested that there was always a motive for the commission of a crime, but sometimes it was impossible to find that motive. He also drew attention to the prisoner having possibly committed the crime without having tried to cover her tracks: this, he suggested, could only be the action of 'a very cunning person'. On the other hand, if she had told her husband on his death bed that she had done her duty by him in fetching medicine and had poisoned him, she was undoubtedly 'a most dreadfully wicked and cunning person'.

However, it was the jury who must decide, by giving due weight and consideration to all the facts.

The only departure from the expected summing up was a note of caution from Justice Bramwell concerning an expression used by the Defence Counsel, which might mislead the jury. Mr Stephen had spoken of 'the absolute certainty of a case', which might be construed by the jury to mean that it could not return a guilty verdict without having that certainty. This was not true: the key concept was one of 'reasonable certainty' which should guide their deliberations. But if the jury did not have that kind of certainty, it should give the prisoner the benefit of the doubt.

The jury retired for ten minutes and returned a verdict of not guilty.

As well as failing to prove the case against Elizabeth Dodds, Mr O'Brien, up against Mr Stephen once again the following day, failed to convince a jury of the innocence of Thomas Richardson on the charge of murder: to be fair, it was a more clear cut case than that involving Mrs Dodds, but it had not been a good two days for him.

The version of the trial reported in the *Louth and North Lincolnshire Advertiser* on the 15th December, on the whole, duplicated that of the *Stamford Mercury*, with the occasional change of words and the inclusion of insignificant additional information. It did depart from both the *Lincolnshire Chronicle* and the *Stamford Mercury*, however, in describing the appearance of Mrs Dodds and her conduct during the Defence Counsel's closing speech. According to the unflattering pen portrait of Mrs Dodds, she was 'a short, stout-built woman of not very prepossessing appearance' who was provided with a seat throughout the trial. Perhaps in an attempt to introduce a sense of drama into a trial in which the jury did not pass a sentence of guilty and the judge did not pass a sentence of death, the reporter noted that the prisoner, throughout the speech of Mr Stephen, 'hid her face and sobbed aloud'. Several other provincial newspapers, published on the same day and later, decided to enhance the manufactured drama by having Mrs Dodds sobbing 'violently' for the duration of the ninety minute speech: which must have been somewhat of a distraction for both Mr Stephen and the jury.

The story of the trial of Elizabeth Dodds appeared in a number of newspapers outside Lincolnshire. These were mainly northern publications which provided a short digest of the trial, using just about enough detail to create a coherent narrative. The editors of the *Manchester Times* and the *Lancaster Gazette* clearly viewed the story as a mere space-filler, distilling it down to four lines in the former and six lines in the latter.

The most curious report of the trial was published on 16th December in *The Era*, a well-established London newspaper. In a lengthy article titled 'Women and Criminal Justice', the writer railed vehemently on 'the dangerous consequences of excepting women from the extreme penalty of the law for their committed crimes and misdeeds'. These consequences were clear: first, a ten-fold increase in the crime of infanticide because of the leniency of the law towards women who murdered their children; secondly, the reluctance of juries to pass a guilty verdict on women, despite the most conclusive evidence. In the view of the newspaper, juries had become mere passive participants in a 'solemn farce' and an 'idle show', when they returned a not guilty verdict to save the prisoner the inconvenience, and the country the expense, of going through a process of reprieve.

An illustration of the failure of juries to do their duty was the recent case of Elizabeth Dodds, accused of poisoning her husband with arsenic. The newspaper provided the reader with an outline of the evidence against Mrs Dodds, including a statistical invention concerning the number of men the quantity of arsenic found in the stomach had the power to kill. In the view of the 'clear circumstantial evidence showing the purchase and possession of poison, the *animus* of the prisoner and other corroborative links', the jury had quite obviously let Mrs Dodds off in order 'to save time and cost'.

The limitation of the astonishingly brutal lament that 'the age of the female execution has gone forever by', was unfortunately later proved wrong in Lincolnshire by the execution of Priscilla Biggadike, in 1868, and of Mary Lefley, in 1884, who both maintained their innocence even as they were being hanged.

The final reference to the trial of Elizabeth Dodds in the media was less scathing than that found in

The Era. The *Sleaford Gazette* had published a short account of the trial on the 15th December which was essentially a truncated re-hash of the lengthy report in the *Lincolnshire Chronicle*. Its final word on the matter, however, was a piece of lightweight seasonal journalism, published on 22nd December, titled 'Lusus Naturae'. The freak of nature in question related to the curious Lincolnshire folklore allegedly cited by Mrs Dodds to justify the claim that her husband was about to die. The article sensibly pointed out that fruit trees flowering twice in the same year signifying an imminent death was 'an absurd superstition'. Rather more harshly, the writer of the article attributed belief in such an idea to the 'ignorance and low moral condition of the districts in which the superstition prevails'.

The unvarnished contempt of the urban sophisticates and cognoscenti of Sleaford for the quaint ways of the rural poor perhaps explains why Harriet Adams was so eager to dissociate herself from such fanciful notions during the trial of Mrs Dodds.

Appendix

Key Players In The Elizabeth Dodds Story

ADAM, Dr Adam Mercer. Surgeon. Gave evidence at the inquest and resumed inquest into the death of John Dodds; and at the trial of Elizabeth Dodds, at the Lincoln Assizes. Resident of Boston.

ADAMS, Harriet. Gave evidence at the inquest and resumed inquest into the death of John Dodds; and at the trial of Elizabeth Dodds, at the Lincoln Assizes. Resident of Claxey Common, Friskney.

ALLENBY, J (Junior). Served on the Grand Jury at the trial of Elizabeth Dodds at the Lincoln Assizes. Resident of Aswell Lane, Louth.

ALLENBY, Samuel. Served on the Grand Jury at the

trial of Elizabeth Dodds at the Lincoln Assizes. Resident of Cadwell Hall.

BERGNE-COUPLAND, Richard. Served on the Grand Jury at the trial of Elizabeth Dodds at the Lincoln Assizes. Resident of Skellingthorpe Hall.

BLAKE, Sarah. Alias Sarah Laming. Gave evidence at the resumed inquest into the death of John Dodds; and at the trial of Elizabeth Dodds, at the Lincoln Assizes.

BROMHEAD, John. Served on the Grand Jury at the trial of Elizabeth Dodds at the Lincoln Assizes. Resident of the Close, Lincoln.

CAMMACK, Dr Richard. Surgeon. Gave evidence at the inquest and resumed inquest into the death of John Dodds; and at the trial of Elizabeth Dodds, at the Lincoln Assizes. Resident of Benington.

CHAPLIN, Lieutenant-Colonel Thomas. Served on the Grand Jury at the trial of Elizabeth Dodds at the Lincoln Assizes. Resident of Blankney Hall.

CHERRINGTON, Henry. Grocer and draper. Resident of Leake.

CRACROFT-AMCOTTS, Colonel Weston. Served on the Grand Jury at the trial of Elizabeth Dodds at the Lincoln Assizes. Resident of Hackthorn Hall.

CRANE, Joseph. Labourer. Lodger with John and Elizabeth Dodds. Gave evidence at the inquest and resumed inquest into the death of John

Dodds; and at the trial of Elizabeth Dodds, at the Lincoln Assizes.

CRANE, Susan. Lodger with John and Elizabeth Dodds. Gave evidence at the inquest and resumed inquest into the death of John Dodds; and at the trial of Elizabeth Dodds, at the Lincoln Assizes.

DIXON, Thomas John. Served on the Grand Jury at the trial of Elizabeth Dodds at the Lincoln Assizes. Resident of Holton Hall.

DODDS, Elizabeth. Arraigned for the wilful murder of her husband, John Dodds. Resident of Wrangle.

DODDS, John. Husband of Elizabeth Dodds. Died of arsenic poisoning. Resident of Wrangle.

EMERIS, William Robert. Served on the Grand Jury at the trial of Elizabeth Dodds at the Lincoln Assizes. Resident of Westgate, Louth.

GARFIT, Thomas. Banker. Resident of Boston.

GILBERT, Sergeant George William. County Constabulary. Gave evidence at the inquest and resumed inquest into the death of John Dodds; and at the trial of Elizabeth Dodds, at the Lincoln Assizes.

GLEED, Richard. Served on the Grand Jury at the trial of Elizabeth Dodds at the Lincoln Assizes. Resident of The Park, Donington.

GREENFIELD, Elizabeth. Gave (inadmissible) evidence at the trial of Elizabeth Dodds, at the Lincoln Assizes. Resident of Wrangle.

HORREY, William. Apprentice to Henry Cherrington, Leake. Gave evidence at the inquest and resumed inquest into the death of John Dodds; and at the trial of Elizabeth Dodds, at the Lincoln Assizes.

HOYLES, Samuel. Gave evidence at the trial of Elizabeth Dodds at the Lincoln Assizes. Resident of Claxey Common, Friskney.

JARVIS, George Knowles. Served on the Grand Jury at the trial of Elizabeth Dodds at the Lincoln Assizes. Resident of Doddington Hall.

LEACHMAN, Robert. Agricultural labourer. Gave evidence at the resumed inquest into the death of John Dodds; and at the trial of Elizabeth Dodds, at the Lincoln Assizes. Resident of Wrangle Bank.

LITTLE, John Caruthers. Coroner at inquest at the Angel Inn, Wrangle, and resumed inquest, into the death of John Dodds. Resident of Boston.

MANTON, Superintendent Thomas. Gave evidence at the inquest and resumed inquest into the death of John Dodds; and at the trial of Elizabeth Dodds, at the Lincoln Assizes.

MELVILLE, Honourable Alexander Leslie. Banker. Served as Foreman on Grand Jury at the trial of Elizabeth Dodds at the Lincoln Assizes. Resident of Branston Hall.

MELVILLE, Alexander Samuel Leslie. Banker. Served on the Grand Jury at the trial of Elizabeth Dodds at the Lincoln Assizes. Resident of Branston Hall.

MONSON, William John, MP. Served on the Grand Jury at the trial of Elizabeth Dodds at the Lincoln Assizes. Resident of Burton Hall.

MOORE, Reverend G A. Served on the Grand Jury at the trial of Elizabeth Dodds at the Lincoln Assizes.

MOORE, Major Charles Thomas John. Served on the Grand Jury at the trial of Elizabeth Dodds at the Lincoln Assizes. Resident of Frampton Hall.

O'BRIEN, _____ Counsel for the Prosecution at the trial of Elizabeth Dodds at the Lincoln Assizes.

PACKE, George Hussey, MP. Served on the Grand Jury at the trial of Elizabeth Dodds at the Lincoln Assizes. Resident of Caythorpe Hall.

PARKER, William. Served on the Grand Jury at the trial of Elizabeth Dodds at the Lincoln Assizes. Resident of Hanthorpe House

PEACOCK, Reverend Wilkinson Affleck. Served on the Grand Jury at the trial of Elizabeth Dodds at the Lincoln Assizes. Resident of Rectory House, Ulceby.

REEVE, Lieutenant-Colonel John (Junior). Served on the Grand Jury at the trial of Elizabeth Dodds at the Lincoln Assizes. Resident of Leadenham House.

SHORT, John Hassard. Served on the Grand Jury at the trial of Elizabeth Dodds at the Lincoln Assizes. Resident of Edlington.

STEPHEN, James Fitzjames. Counsel for the Defence at the trial of Elizabeth Dodds at the Lincoln Assizes.

WALDO-SIBTHORP, Gervaise Tottenham, MP. Served on the Grand Jury at the trial of Elizabeth Dodds at the Lincoln Assizes. Resident of Canwick Hall, Lincoln.

WILLSON, Anthony. Served on the Grand Jury at the trial of Elizabeth Dodds at the Lincoln Assizes. Resident of Rauceby Hall.

WILSHERE, Honourable George William, Baron Bramwell. Presiding judge at the trial of Elizabeth Dodds at the Lincoln Assizes.

Chapter Three

Ellen Green (1842-?)

Ellen Green: Timeline

1842: Eleanor Dickinson, daughter of Robert and Mary Dickinson, born in Sibsey.

1862: Marriage of Eleanor Dickinson, aged twenty, to Thomas Green, aged twenty-four, at Boston.

1871: Ellen, Thomas and George Green, son, aged eight, resident at Kyme Tower, Boston.

13th May, 1875: Dr James Edward Tuxford receives message to attend the home of Thomas and Ellen Green, at Fishtoft, where he found both adults and their son, George, ill from arsenic poisoning; attended in the afternoon, also, by Dr Arthur Tuxford.

House searched by Sergeant Thomas Henson.

14th May, 1875: house searched a second time by Sergeant Henson; the dying declaration of Thomas Green taken in front of a magistrate, his clerk and Superintendent Thoresby.

14th-16th May: family attended by Dr James and Dr Arthur Tuxford, as Thomas Green deteriorates, George Green slowly recovers and Ellen Green makes a full recovery.

17th May, 1875: death of Thomas Green between 8 o'clock and 8.30 in the morning.

Adjourned inquest at Fishtoft into the death of Edward Green, at 6 o'clock in the evening, presided over by Dr Walter Clegg, at the house of John Allen.

19th May, 1875: burial of Thomas Green at St Guthlac's Church, Fishtoft; arrest of Ellen Green and taken to Skirbeck Quarter lock-up.

20th May, 1875: Ellen Green appears before Boston magistrate and remanded in custody.

21st May, 1875: John Bonnett arrested.

25th May, 1875: hearing into the death of Thomas Green, in front of Lieutenant-Colonel Charles Moore and Thomas Garfit at Boston Sessions House. Committal of Ellen Green for trial at Lincoln Assizes.

26th May, 1875: Ellen Green taken by rail to Spalding gaol by Sergeant Henson.

2nd June, 1875: Ellen Green received at Lincoln Castle to await trial.

25th July, trial of Ellen Green, in front of Baron

Nathaniel Lindley, for the wilful murder of her husband, Thomas Green. Found Not Guilty by a Grand Jury and acquitted.

'The Most Diabolical Crime And Most Cruel Murder': The Acquittal Of Ellen Green

After their acquittal, it seems that both Jane Bell and Elizabeth Dodds slipped quietly back into obscurity and the silences of history.

Jane Bell left the Assize court in Lincoln a free woman, although perhaps a little apprehensive after the experience of having been found Not Guilty at a Coroner's court in Laceby, only to be rearrested a few days afterwards.

She briefly resurfaced six years later in the 1851 Census for Raithby cum Maltby, two miles from Louth, as a visitor at the house of William Wright, a shepherd. Recorded as a widow, she was accompanied by two sons, James Bell, aged nine and John Bell, aged four years old.

Elizabeth Dodds left the Assize court having exchanged the prospect of a fearful public meeting with the hangman for the less harrowing experience of private anonymity and insignificance, thanks mainly to the sharp rhetorical skills of the Counsel for the Defence and a limp performance from the Prosecution.

A few months later, according to the 1861 Census, she was living in Corpus Christi Lane, Boston, with another widow, Jane Simpson, a fifty-three year old charwoman. Her occupation is listed as laundress, living with her two children, Thomas Dodds, aged four and Edward Dodds, aged two. Edward was the infant who had been removed to the workhouse during the incarceration of Mrs Dodds while awaiting trial.

These quiet exits from Lincoln Castle contrast markedly with that of Mrs Ellen Green of Fishtoft, two miles from Boston, who on the 25th July, 1875, was acquitted of poisoning her husband with arsenic. Accompanied by her two sisters, Mrs Green would have preferred a similarly discreet exit from the Castle, no doubt, but unfortunately some of the citizens of Lincoln had other ideas.

The whole unsavoury episode of Ellen Green's exit from court was reported by the *Lincolnshire Chronicle* of Friday, 30th July. Intending to leave the city for Boston, via the Great Northern Railway Station, Mrs Green had managed to get as far as the top of Steep Hill, just beyond the Castle, 'without molestation or interference'. Things turned ugly, however, when 'a self-important passer-by' pointed Mrs Green out to the crowd of people who were also descending the hill. The newspaper speculated that the person in question was either someone who had been present during Ellen Green's trial, or even worse, was possibly one of those people 'who behaved indecorously in court'.

The reaction of the people on the street was to

hiss and hoot at Mrs Green, with matters spiralling out of control near the Magpies Inn, on Watergate North, where she was threatened with physical violence. Despite the best efforts of 'better disposed persons', Mrs Green had to be rescued by a number of policemen, who took her to the relative safety of a house in Jackson's Court. It proved to be only a temporary solution to the problem, however, as an unruly mob of 'roughs' surrounded the house and threatened to burn it down should Mrs Green be allowed to remain there.

In response to the imminent danger to life and property from the threatened robust action of the citizenry, the police managed to smuggle Mrs Green out of the house and into an omnibus, which took her to the end of Washingborough Road on the city outskirts, from where she walked back to the house in Jackson's Court, and stayed there all night.

In the end, she managed to leave Lincoln the following morning, on the 6.30 train, although not before being subject to further hissing at the station.

The report ended with the hope that 'the roughs engaged in these unseemly demonstrations' were not inhabitants of 'our peaceable and well-ordered town', concluding that such conduct 'may be Briton like, but it is the reverse of manly'.

It was a soothing and comfortable image of the city created for the reader, but one which conveniently forgot about such alarming disturbances as the borough election riot of February, 1874, which involved a large mob of Lincoln citizens, armed with catapults and bricks, fighting a pitched battle on the High Street with the 91st Regiment, which had been summoned from Manchester by the city magistrates after a reading of the Riot Act.

It is not difficult to account for public hostility towards Ellen Green: from the point at which the story first broke in the *Boston Guardian and Lincolnshire Independent* newspaper on the 15th May, 1875, to the final speech by the Counsel for the Prosecution at the Assize court on the 25th July, there is a strong sense that any outcome other than the death penalty would have been the wrong one as far as popular opinion was concerned. The circumstantial evidence of a cunningly hatched plot to kill off her husband with arsenic whilst recklessly endangering the life of her son, the strong suspicion that she was involved in a shameless adulterous relationship with a younger man and her alleged brazen attempts to influence witness statements and pervert the course of justice, created a toxic image of ruthless criminality.

Headlined 'A Family Poisoned near Boston', the initial report in the Boston newspaper of the 15th May was innocuously sandwiched between the story of a failed suicide attempt outside the church at Frampton West and a helpful list of the times of the Sunday services in the town's many places of worship. At this point, it was just a developing story, consisting of a compound of loosely related facts and speculation, plus just enough restrained sensationalism to engage the reader's attention.

Shortly after 8 o'clock on the Thursday morning of 13th May, a messenger had arrived at the surgery of Boston surgeon, James Edward Tuxford, with an urgent request to attend a family by the name of Green, who were residing near Hawthorn Tree, located on the Low Road to Frieston.

On arriving at the house, the doctor discovered that all three members of the household – the father, the mother and the young son – were showing symptoms of having ingested an irritant poison. It emerged, on questioning, that these symptoms began soon after breakfast, specifically, after having drunk a cup of tea.

All three were given an unspecified treatment for arsenic poisoning, probably an emetic, and Dr Tuxford remained with the family to monitor their progress. After a couple of hours, he departed, taking with him a pitcher of water from the kettle used to make the tea. The sample of water was later analysed by his son, Dr Arthur Tuxford, who found a large quantity of arsenic in it.

Dr Arthur Tuxford later went to check on the Green family and remained for the entire afternoon, giving them 'such remedies as the patients demanded', before going back to Boston.

Dr Edward Tuxford returned in the evening to discover that Mr Green's condition had significantly deteriorated, which contrasted with that of the young boy, who was still very ill, but improving, and his wife, who had just about made a full recovery. The following day, on visiting the house again, he found Mr Green in a critical state and with little hope of recovery.

The information, almost entirely focused on a harrowing couple of days in the lives of two well-known Boston doctors, was supplemented by the assurance that the police were currently investigating the matter. In an unusually discreet statement of principle, the newspaper therefore thought it would 'not be prudent to make any remarks on the matter'. However, clearly struggling to be prudent, the story ended by sharing with its readers a couple of the many rumours about the case which were already doing the rounds in the area.

First, it was rumoured that the husband drank four cups of tea, whilst his wife drank less than one, which 'fully accounted' for the man being much worse than the woman. The second rumour which the report was happy to share was that a kettle had been left outside the house overnight and someone had put arsenic in it.

Inquest Into The Death Of Thomas Green, Held At The House Of Mr John Allen, Fishtoft, Monday 17th May, 1875

Sensing that it might be on to yet another sensational Lincolnshire poisoning story, the *Boston Guardian and Lincolnshire Independent* of the 22nd May reported on the inquest into the death of Mr Green in detail. The newspaper provided its readers with an impressive depth of coverage, as well as an equally impressive extended prejudicial new headline: 'The Family Poisoning Case. Death of Husband, Inquest on the Body, and Apprehension of the Widow and her Alleged Paramour'.

Thomas Green had died on the morning of Monday 17th May; by early evening, Dr Walter Clegg, the highly regarded Boston Coroner, had convened an inquest at the house of John Allen, a local farmer, resident of Wythe Lane, Fishtoft. The speed and efficiency of the organisation of the inquest was impressive, although the Coroner was clear that there would have to be an adjournment to allow the police to gather further evidence.

After the swearing in of the jury, Dr Clegg opened the inquest with a review of the information which was currently in his possession. He informed the court that on the previous Thursday, Thomas Green had been struck down by 'intense pain and other symptoms', which had suggested 'an illness of an unusual nature'. The treatment of the deceased by Dr James Edward Tuxford had been prompt and carried out with 'great judgement and discretion', as he had retrieved a sample of water used to make the breakfast tea, as well as other suspect matter.

As Dr Tuxford had discovered arsenic in the sample of water, it was the duty of the jury to ascertain, based upon the evidence they would hear, whether Thomas Green had died from accidental poisoning, suicide or deliberate poison by another hand.

Walter Clegg was an experienced Coroner who was well aware of the potential difficulties posed for a jury by prejudicial rumour and gossip, especially in cases relating to death by poison: it was a concern which he was still voicing nine years later at the inquest into the death of William Lefley in Wrangle, which led eventually to the hanging of Mary Lefley, his wife.

Dr Clegg therefore highlighted to the jury that he was aware of 'many painful rumours' circulating round the district and expressed the hope that they would be proved to be without foundation. In a memorable summary of the purpose of an inquest, he insisted that whilst the process was 'due to the dead', it was 'of much more importance to the living'.

After the identification of the body, a number of witnesses were heard.

The first witness to appear was the splendidly named Esmeranda Rowson, who had lived next door to Thomas Green for over a year. Mrs Rowson had been returning from milking at around 8 o'clock on the previous Thursday when she saw Ellen Green standing by her door. She was told by her that the whole family was ill and that Thomas Green was especially 'bad', something which she discovered for herself when she found him lying in the yard against a straw-stack in great pain and vomiting. He was also complaining of a burning sensation in his throat and chest, as well as sweating profusely.

Mrs Rowson confirmed that Mr and Mrs Green lived on good terms with each other, along with their son, and that she had never heard them quarrel.

She ended her deposition by saying that on the Thursday afternoon and night, she had witnessed both Mrs Green and her son also being very ill.

Sarah Stopper, the sister of Mrs Green, deposed that she had turned up at the house around 8 o'clock on the Thursday morning to help with the ironing, as well as to have breakfast. On discovering that there was no one around, she had gone down the yard, where she discovered all three of the family very ill. Mrs Green had instructed her to fetch the doctor as they were all unwell after drinking some tea. Confirming the narrative of Mrs Rowson, she set off to Boston for the doctor, but returned after hearing that a messenger had already been sent. She ended her deposition by also confirming that her sister and her husband had been on the best of terms.

Regular readers of the *Boston Guardian and Lincolnshire Independent* would already have had some familiarity with the part played by Dr James Edward Tuxford in the case. His deposition at the inquest, however, added some interesting detail to the general outline previously reported in the newspaper. In contrast to the rumoured four cups of tea, Mr Green had only drunk a cup and a half, before feeling very ill. Mrs Green, who told the doctor that she had also been sick, had only drunk half a cup of tea: in the opinion of Dr Tuxford, Mrs Green had not been seriously ill.

On leaving the house, Dr Tuxford had removed the teapot, along with its contents, the top layer in the sugar basin, as well as the previously reported bottle of water taken from the kettle. He confirmed to the court that his initial analysis of the water had revealed the presence of arsenic.

Thomas Green had died at 8 o'clock on the morning of the 17th May, and he had performed a post mortem on his body: the stomach was inflamed and had presented all the appearances of containing irritant poison. As a consequence, Dr Tuxford had put the viscera into sealed jars, which were now in the custody of the superintendent of police.

He concluded by saying that the son of Thomas Green, a boy of twelve, continued to be ill for a couple of days, whilst his wife 'showed no serious symptoms of poisoning'. She had said that she had been sick several times, but she had not required any medical intervention.

Dr Arthur Tuxford, confirmed that he had supported his father in his treatment of Thomas Green, as well as in the analysis of the water taken from the kettle and the post mortem examination. He had been present when the sealed jars were handed over to Superintendent John Thoresby.

Ellen Green had been 'strongly cautioned' by the Coroner concerning the possible legal consequences of speaking at the inquest - however, she had chosen to ignore the advice and deposed.

Mrs Green recounted having breakfast with her husband and son, when they were all three 'seized with pain and sickness'. They thought that it was the tea which had made them ill; specifically, she thought that it was the tea which had burned her throat. Her husband went outside and she had followed him. She recalled that he had drunk 'a large breakfast cupful and a half', whilst the cups used by her and her son were only small teacups.

The water used to make the tea had been taken from the pump in the yard, as was normal, and was boiled in the kettle 'we have used for years'. The kettle had been left outside, next to the pump overnight, at about 5 o'clock in the evening of Wednesday, 12th May. Mrs Green was insistent that she had seen white mercury many years ago, whilst in service, but there had never been any in the house since she was married. Whilst Ellen Green, formerly Eleanor Dickinson of Sibsey, did not specify any dates in her deposition, the time frame in question was quite a long one, having married Thomas Green in 1862.

As far as she was aware, Mrs Green claimed that she did not have any enemies who might have put poison in the kettle.

The voice of twelve year old George Green was the next to be heard in front of the jury. He confirmed that he had been taken ill at the same time as his father and mother, and also that he had 'never heard of any poison being used in our house for vermin'. The young boy's account of the kettle was not entirely conclusive: he did not know what had been done with the kettle after tea on the Wednesday evening; it was often stood outside all night, but he did not see it next to the pump when he was out in the yard. Initially, whilst sitting down to breakfast, he had been at the table with his father, whilst his mother was busy in another part of the house: she had joined them after about three or four minutes. George Green did not drink a full cup of tea and when he began to feel ill, he went outside with his parents; his mother had instructed them not to drink any more as there was something wrong with the tea.

At this point, the Coroner invited the jury to consider the evidence which they had so far heard. He advised them that there could be no doubt that Thomas Green had died from the effects of arsenic poisoning, and that the water boiled in the kettle for breakfast contained the deadly substance. If they took the evidence of Mrs Green to be true, that the kettle had been left out all night, it was impossible to reach a conclusion of accidental poisoning. In short, 'the most diabolical crime and most cruel murder' had been committed by someone.

However, Dr Clegg wished to remain cautious until further evidence was forthcoming, and adjourned the inquest until 6 o'clock on the following Monday.

The *Lincolnshire Chronicle* had also sensed that a sensational story was unfolding near Boston and reported on the initial inquest in detail. The report was published on Friday, 21st May, the day before that of the *Boston and Lincolnshire Independent*, although without any reference to the subsequent developments uncovered by the Boston newspaper. It may be that the Lincoln publication was aware of these unsavoury developments, but chose to take the moral high ground when it stated that 'various rumours respecting this sad affair are circulated, but we simply give the evidence taken before the Coroner'.

A comparison between the two newspaper accounts of the inquest occasionally provides additional information. The messenger who alerted Dr Tuxford was the groom of a Mr Porter; on his initial visit to the house, Dr Tuxford had administered an emetic to the deceased; and Mrs Rowson had stated that she had known Thomas Green for six or seven years.

Of greater significance, perhaps, was that Mrs Rowson had described seeing Mrs Green being sick several times in the afternoon, as well as being 'very bad at night', which was somewhat at odds with the opinion of Dr Tuxford. Further, an expanded version of the deposition of Ellen Green concerning the possession of arsenic was slightly different, in that she said that there had been vermin killer in the house 'about a month ago', but her husband had been in charge of it.

The sensational headline in the *Boston Guardian and Lincolnshire Independent* which preceded the report of the inquest referred to the 'apprehension of the widow and her alleged paramour'. Of course, the inquest had no knowledge of these developments, but the newspaper was more than happy to clarify matters for its readers, with an appended paragraph.

Thomas Green had been buried on Wednesday, 19th May, and immediately after the funeral Ellen Green was apprehended and taken to the police station at Skirbeck Quarter. She was brought before the magistrate on the following day and remanded in custody until Saturday, 22nd May. In the course of Thursday, 20th May, a young man named Bonnett, reported to be the paramour of Mrs Green, was also arrested, on suspicion of having colluded with her in the death of her husband. The latest information on Bonnett was that until recently he had been a servant in the employment of a farmer living close to Mrs Green, and that the couple had been 'more intimate than they ought to have been'. Bonnett was reported to have left the neighbourhood and had since been employed as a trolley man by the Great Northern Railway Company.

This latest intelligence ended with the claim that Bonnett and Mrs Green had been seen in Lincoln together the previous month and that the poison had been purchased there.

Hearing Related To The Murder Of Thomas Green, Sessions House, Boston, Tuesday, 25th June. 1875

The resumed inquest proposed by Dr Clegg was made redundant by the circumstances leading to the arrest of Mrs Green and John Bonnett, and their subsequent appearance in front of magistrates Lieutenant-Colonel Charles Moore and Thomas Garfit, charged with the wilful murder of Thomas Green of Fishtoft, cottager, by means of arsenic poisoning.

According to the *Lincolnshire Chronicle,* published on the 4th June, the administration of the case had not been straightforward. Originally, it was going to be heard in private, in the Grand Jury Room at the Sessions House, until Thomas Garfit had intervened and insisted it be heard in open court.

The packed hearing was reported extensively by the *Lincolnshire Chronicle* and the *Boston Guardian and Lincolnshire Independent*; perhaps sensing the unhappiest of endings for the two accused, it was also reported by the *Stamford Mercury*.

The case for the Prosecution was represented by Mr C Bean; Ellen Green was represented by Mr Benjamin Bissell Dyer and John Bonnett by Mr W H Bailes: all three were Boston solicitors. The seriousness of the case was emphasised by the presence of Captain Philip Bicknell, Chief Constable of Lincolnshire.

The opening of the hearing was a brisk one, with Mr Bean simply stating that he had been instructed to prosecute the charge of murder against 'the woman Green', but would not be entering into making a statement: he preferred to leave matters in the capable hands of the Bench.

The information which had been gathered against both prisoners was read out by Superintendent Thoresby, before the witnesses were called.

Sarah Stopper, wife of William Stopper, labourer, of Frieston, and sister of Mrs Green, was the first to depose. Her statement was largely a repetition of what was heard at the inquest, with the additional information that ironing the linen for her sister was an established Tuesday and Thursday arrangement. She also told the court that when she returned from her aborted journey to Boston to call the doctor, she found that her sister and Mrs Rowson had managed to get Thomas Green into his bed. Further, she had decided to stay with her sister overnight.

Mr Dyer's questioning of Sarah Stopper was clearly intended to establish that Mrs Green had been seriously ill: she confirmed that Ellen Green had vomited 'on and off all day at intervals', as did her son, George. Mrs Green had attempted to assist her husband during the course of the day, but had been limited by her own illness. The report in the *Stamford Mercury* added that according to Mrs Stopper her sister had spent most of the day lying on the couch. Probably in reply to another question from Mr Dyer she said, 'I can't say who was the worst'.

In response to Mr Bailes, Mrs Stopper confirmed that John Bonnett was not present in the house that day.

Sarah Stopper concluded, as she had done at the inquest, by stating that Mr and Mrs Green lived on good terms with each other.

Esmeranda Rowson, wife of Thomas Rowson, a cottager of Boston, had also presented important eye-witness evidence at the inquest. As with Sarah Stopper, she repeated the same story, with the occasional new detail, such as her having lived next door to Thomas Green and having been on friendly terms with both Mr and Mrs Green. She also added to the deposition heard at the inquest a conversation she had with Ellen Green on first discovering the family ill in the yard. In response to her questioning Mrs Green about the cause of their illness, and specifically about the sugar she had used in her tea, she replied that she had used the same tea and sugar as usual, adding that the kettle had been out all night.

The most interesting part of her deposition related to John Bonnett and his relationship to Ellen Green, concerning which Mrs Rowson seemed to have a good deal of information for the Bench to consider.

Mrs Rowson had once travelled to Lincoln Fair with Ellen Green and her son, and had been joined on the train by her husband's aunt and uncle, as well as by John Bonnett. Whilst at Lincoln, they had all gone into a dancing room. The previous July, Mrs Rowson had gone to Skegness on a Saturday afternoon and had arranged with Ellen Green to meet her there on the following day. Mrs Green had arrived in Skegness on the Sunday and was accompanied by John Bonnett and another young man, who was Mrs Rowson's lodger at the time: she added that Thomas Green was not with her.

Mr Bailes, not surprisingly, did not express any interest whatsoever in his client's outings to Lincoln and Skegness, preferring to ask Mrs Rowson to confirm that John Bonnett was not present at the house on the day of the poisoning, which she did. Predictably, Mr Dyer pressed Mrs Rowson to confirm that Ellen Green was very ill on that day: repeating the words she had used at the inquest, Esmeranda Rowson confirmed that her friend and former close neighbour 'was vomiting a great deal in the afternoon and night'. Perhaps sensing a possible weakness in the testimony, Mr Bean tried to establish a clear timeline relating to the administration of medicine by Dr Tuxford and Mrs Green vomiting. Mrs Rowson's reply was not especially helpful in that she said that Mrs Green vomited both before and after taking medicine, and that she had been sick at some point after dinner.

George Green, the son of the deceased and Ellen Green, was keen to inform the court that he was thirteen years old next November, before moving on to his deposition. The testimony of the boy was much sharper and clearer than it had been at the inquest and had a very particular focus upon the tea provided for him and his father at breakfast. His mother had prepared breakfast before he had got up; he and his father had sat down together at the table as the tea had already been made; the tea was poured and they drank it whilst Mrs Green was out of the room. He drank about three quarters from a small cup, whilst his father had about a cup and a half from a large cup. His mother returned to the room after his father had drunk the first cup of tea and was starting to drink the second cup. At this point, his father left the room, feeling ill. His mother had a small cup and drank about three quarters of it, before she too became ill, and followed his father outside. His father had laid himself down on the straw and had been sick, whilst his mother sat beside him and he stood against them. George said that both he and his mother were sick.

After the arrival of the doctor, he took some medicine, but he was not sure if his mother had taken any.

Up to this point, young George's testimony had been a detailed expansion of what he had deposed at the inquest. The final part of his deposition, however, was completely new and created an insistently sentimental picture of domestic harmony in the midst of tragedy. Both George and his mother were present in the bedroom when Thomas Green was on the point of death, at 8 o'clock on the morning of 17th May. He heard his father say something to his mother: he did not say what it was, but it was said 'in love, not in anger'.

Mr Dyer's questions to George were interested in

him confirming that the eating of breakfast whilst his mother was out of the room was routine and that the leaving of the kettle outside the door at night was a frequent occurrence: the boy agreed that this was the case on both counts.

The evidence of Dr James Tuxford was in part a repetition of his account of the circumstances of his attending Thomas Green and his family, which had been heard at the inquest. In addition, he provided fresh details relating to his treatment and also the relative severity of illness. In his opinion, Mrs Green had not shown the same symptoms as her husband and son and he had therefore not given her any medicine to take: he had given Thomas and George Green an emetic, but had not thought it necessary to give the same to Ellen Green.

After reminding the court that he had carried out the necessary post mortem which had confirmed the presence of arsenic in the stomach of the deceased, Dr Tuxford moved on from mundane fact to extraordinary anecdote.

On Saturday 15th May, he was at the house when a magistrate was recording a dying declaration from Thomas Green. Sarah Stopper, the sister of Mrs Green, was also in the house and was listening at the bedroom door, as the magistrate went about his business. Dr Tuxford took Mrs Stopper away and distracted her from what was being said.

Surprisingly, this suspicious detail was not included in the report of the *Stamford Mercury*.

There appeared to have been no follow up to the revelation, other than Colonel Moore asking Dr Tuxford to confirm that he did not attend Ellen Green. Dr Tuxford confirmed this and added that it was Mrs Green who had told him that she had been sick. In the version of Dr Tuxford's reply to the question reported in the *Boston Guardian and Lincolnshire Independent*, he added that he did not see Mrs Green vomit, 'although there was some matter that appeared to have been ejected from the stomach beside her.'

The deposition of Dr Arthur Tuxford at the inquest had been a more or less routine one of confirming that he had assisted his father in his work. Following on from the testimony of Dr Edward Tuxford, he now provided new information relating to the apparent illness of Mrs Green and its treatment. Interestingly, the account of his visit to the house on the 13th May was closer in some respects to that reported in the *Boston Guardian and Lincolnshire Independent* of the 15th May than that heard at the inquest.

In this latest version of Arthur Tuxford's involvement, his deposition focused more on Ellen Green than on the deceased. He had seen all three members of the Green family, but only the father and the son he considered to be very ill. He had seen Mrs Green, who had told him that she was very ill and had been sick. In line with his father, Arthur Tuxford's prognosis was that Mrs Green showed no symptoms of arsenic poisoning. She had complained to him that she was in pain and had been sick, and so he had given her some medicine and had ordered a mustard plaster to ease the pain. He had quite naturally asked to examine Mrs Green's vomit, had she had been sick, but had been told that Mrs Stopper had thrown it away. He confirmed to the court that the medicine which he had given to Mrs Green would have made her sick.

Arthur Tuxford ended this part of his deposition by saying that Mrs Green had asked him to attend her, rather than his father. It was remark which was open to interpretation, but never pursued.

At this point in the proceedings, the only witnesses to depose had been those heard at the inquest. The witnesses who followed presented an array of different perspectives, many of them hostile to Ellen Green.

John Thomas Moore, a Boston greengrocer, had met up with Thomas Green in Boston on Wednesday, 12th May, and had arranged to cut some cabbages for him, deliver them the next day and have breakfast with him. He had arrived at 9 o'clock, too late for breakfast, and had been surprised to see Dr Tuxford's trap outside the house. Mr Moore had discreetly waited until the doctor had departed before going into the house. He had, however, spoken to Mrs Green outside the house and had enquired what was the matter: she made no reply and went back into the house. When Mr Moore went inside after the doctor had left, he had found Thomas Green lying fully clothed in his bed, with his wife in the room and the boy on a sofa in another room. He had asked Thomas Green what had happened, who replied, ' I'm done, they have done me', but did not mention any names. Mr Moore did not clarify whether or not Ellen Green was in the room at the time.

What he did make clear was that he had observed Thomas Green and his son being sick, but not Mrs Green: neither did he hear her complain about being sick, although he did say that he was only in the house for about half an hour.

He had returned to the house the following day, when Mr Green, in the presence of his wife, had said, 'I can't understand it why I should be poisoned on my own premises, hope the right party will be found out and justly punished for what they have done to me'.

Mr Moore had also had a conversation with Mrs Green in the presence of her husband. She had explained to him the drinking of the tea by Mr Green and how ill it had made him, as it had both her and George. She had followed her husband outside and had been sick herself; also, she returned to the house to prevent her son drinking any more tea. After telling

Mr Moore that she had called a neighbour for help, she also let him know, as she had several people, that the kettle had been outside all night, near the pump.

Mr Dyer had realised the potential difficulties which Mr Moore's evidence had produced and therefore questioned him: in response, he said that he knew the couple very well and had never known them to quarrel. The version in the *Stamford Mercury* was a little more expansive and useful to Mr Dyer's attempt to nullify problematic interpretations of his words by the jury. Mr Moore had traded a good deal with Thomas Green for over three years and had been a frequent visitor to the house. Further, he described himself as having been 'intimately acquainted with the family', as well as confirming that they had lived happily as man and wife.

John Thomas Moore was followed by John Ostler, a cottager residing in Skirbeck, who had accompanied Sergeant Henson to the house on the 13th May. They had arrived at 5 o'clock: the policeman was clearly trying to establish some preliminary facts concerning what had happened. They had found Thomas Green and his son very ill in bed, whilst Ellen Green was seated on the sofa downstairs in the company of Mrs Stopper. Sergeant Henson had asked Mrs Green precisely what had happened to cause the illness of her husband and son, but Mrs Green said that she did not know. In response to the sergeant's question about having poison in the house, she said that there had been mouse poison in the house three months ago, of which half had been used to kill the vermin and the unused half had been burnt by her husband. She also said that she believed that poison had been put in the kettle or in the nozzle of the water pump.

On the same day, Mrs Green had revealed to John Ostler that it was a 'lucky job' that her sister did not end up being poisoned as well. She had described herself running up the yard and crying out to her sister, 'Good God, don't drink it, there's arsenic or poison in it, which has made us all ill together'. The dramatic intervention to prevent Mrs Stopper from drinking a cup of tea which she had poured herself from the breakfast table, rather surprisingly, had not been mentioned by her, in either of her depositions: neither was it reported by the *Stamford Mercury*.

John Ostler had, however, mentioned the conversation to Sergeant Henson.

If the short deposition of John Ostler placed question marks against the truthfulness of Ellen Green, that of his wife, Eliza Ostler, raised questions about her sensitivity and awareness of the gravity of the situation. Mrs Ostler had also visited the house on the 13th May to express her sympathy and to ask what had happened. Mrs Green was lying on the sofa 'apparently ill' and recounted her story of arsenic in the kettle. Her second visit, at 4 o'clock in the morning, was on the 17th May, the day that Thomas Green had died. Mrs Ostler had expressed the opinion to Ellen Green that her husband was dying, to which she had allegedly replied, somewhat brusquely, 'I can't help it, I have not done it'.

The testimony of Frederick Swain, a labourer resident in Skirbeck, as reported in the newspaper, was an interesting miscellany of anecdotes based upon his visit to see Mr Green on the 17th May, just a couple of hours before he died. Mr Green was lying in bed and his wife and son were lying on a different bed in the same room. Also in the bedroom were the brother and sister of Thomas Green, who presumably had also come to say their farewells to the dying man.

After setting the scene, Mr Swain then recounted an astonishing story which was somewhat at odds with George Green's touching narrative of his parents' last moments together. According to Mr Swain, Ellen Green had asked her husband to give her a kiss, but he had told her that he did not want to kiss her. Mrs Green, however, kissed her husband and then had asked him a second and third time to kiss her. It seems that Thomas Green only relented when his sister said, 'Give her a kiss, lovey'. Unfortunately, any semblance of domestic harmony was destroyed when Mrs Green tried to cover her husband's feet: his response, according to Mr Swain, was to swear at her, at which point, Mrs Green ran out of the room crying.

The less reticent version of the words allegedly spoken by Thomas Green, reported by the *Stamford Mercury*, was in the form of a partial quotation: 'D_____n your eyes. You _____ . The *Boston Guardian and Lincolnshire Independent* was less sparing of its readers, but slightly more helpful in capturing the moment: 'D____ your eyes. You b_____y snot'.

A third interesting version of the outburst, published in the trial report of the *Leicester Daily Post* of the 31st July, reported that Thomas Green had said, 'D_____ your eyes. You _____sot'. That Ellen Green had a drink problem, if that is what was meant, was neither stated nor implied in any of the Lincolnshire reports, although curiously it was noted by the *Nottingham Guardian* of the 31st July that John Thomas Moore deposed that on arriving at the house 'the prisoner was not sober'.

Mr Dyer asked Swain to confirm that Thomas Green's sister was in the room when he swore, which he did, and also confirmed that he had passed details of the unpleasant exchange on to the sergeant. The precise point being made by the solicitor in defence of his client was not made clear in the report.

Mr Swain had provided evidence not entirely to Mrs Green's advantage; it was followed by further revelations which were even more uncomfortable for her. As well as being on friendly terms with Mr and

Mrs Green, Frederick Swain also knew John Bonnett quite well. He had seen Mrs Green and Mr Bonnett together in Boston on market days, including quite recently, on the 5th May, when they were riding on the steam roundabouts as Thomas Green looked on, having apparently having drunk a quantity of alcohol.

If Mr Dyer wasn't feeling slightly uncomfortable at this juncture, he soon would be, as Sergeant Thomas Henson and Police Constable Isaac Raynor, both stationed at Skirbeck, stepped up to give compelling evidence of Mrs Green's tenuous understanding of the concept of truthfulness: a difficulty compounded by her having ignored cautions about her words being used as evidence against her in a court of law.

Sergeant Henson confirmed that he had visited the house, accompanied by John Ostler, at around 5 o'clock on Thursday the 13th May. He had initially spoken to Mrs Stopper and Mrs Green, the latter telling him that the family had been poisoned by arsenic from either the kettle or the pump nozzle. She also told him that she usually left the kettle in the back-house, but for some reason had left it by the pump. The Sergeant had asked about mouse poison and Mrs Green told him that there had been a packet in the house which had been purchase by her husband, who had used half of it and had burnt the rest; as far as arsenic was concerned, they had never had any in the house.

Sergeant Henson had returned to the house on

Friday, the 14th May, when the magistrate, Mr Foster and his clerk were recording a dying declaration from Thomas Green, along with Superintendent Thoresby. When they entered his bedroom, Mrs Green said, 'They have no business to go in there to ask him questions. If they want to know anything I can tell them all they want to know'.

Whilst the declaration was being taken, the prisoner had instructed Mrs Stopper to stand by the door and listen to the questions being asked: she was ushered away by Dr Tuxford.

Once again, the *Stamford Mercury* made no reference to the episode; the *Boston Guardian and Lincolnshire Independent*, on the other hand, reported that Mrs Green did not say anything else after her angry assertions. It also brought the scene to life with the minor detail that Mrs Stopper 'had placed her ear close to the door'.

On the 19th May, Mrs Green was apprehended and taken to the lock-up at Skirbeck Quarter, where Sergeant Henson was in charge of her for a time. She confided in him that she knew Jack Bonnett, who lived with Mr Porter; she knew that he possessed some mercury poison, as he had once nearly killed the horses with it: in her opinion, he would have known where the kettle was left.

Superintendent Thoresby came in and the subject was dropped.

On the 26th May, he had escorted Mrs Green to Spalding gaol and during the journey, she began to make a statement. He had cautioned her that if she did so, he would be obliged to take it down in writing and it could be used against her in court. She ignored his advice and provided him with a short statement. A few days ago, she had seen a brown paper parcel, about two inches long and one inch thick, in a cupboard. Her husband had told her that it was poison and it had no business being in the house. Mrs Green said that if it was poison, she wanted him to take it away so that George did not get hold of it. Her husband had taken it away, but she was not sure what he had done with it. He may have disposed of it in the ash-bin or the petty-hole or had possibly buried it in the garden, near the tubs. Somewhat speculatively, Mrs Green also suggested that he may have taken it round the back of the house and put it in the kettle himself, or it may have ended up in there accidentally. The rather unconvincing guesswork ended with the lame observation that it was 'some white sort of stuff'.

On the same day, on that part of the journey between Spalding railway station and the gaol, she also told the Sergeant that John Bonnett had once or twice asked her to leave her husband and go away with him.

On the 1st June, Sergeant Henson once again had charge of Ellen Green, after she had been brought back to Skirbeck from Spalding gaol by Mrs Bates, the female warder. A further exchange took place at 9 o'clock between the sergeant and Mrs Green, in which she had asked the sergeant, 'how the case was getting on', to which he had replied that, 'it will be fully gone into today'.

She once again wished to make a statement to him and once again was cautioned. Mrs Green was quite insistent that her statement should be heard, and declared with confidential triumph that ' I shall tell the gentlemen the grand secret today'.

She told the sergeant that she went to Boston Fair on the Wednesday, with her husband, and had arranged to meet him later in town at the end of Dolphin Lane, to go home, but did not meet him. Instead, she returned home with Mrs Rowson, and had some tea with her, before returning to the fair. On the Saturday morning before he died, he had called her into the room, as he wished to speak to her. Mrs Allen, the wife of John Allen, and Mrs Rowson were there at the time, and he told them both to leave the room. They both left the room and she shut the door. He confessed to her, 'I have done this myself. I put the arsenic in the kettle when it was boiling on the fire'. In addition, he told her that he tried to do it once before: 'I put it in a pitcher, but my heart misgave me, and I threw it away'. The reason he gave for having put arsenic in the kettle was that he had heard something in Boston 'that I could not bear'.

It was an extraordinary story, only bettered by the deposition which followed from PC Isaac Raynor. He had been on duty at the inquest into the death of Thomas Green at the house of Mr Allen. Sarah Stopper was called to give evidence to the court and on her way in Mrs Green had said to her, 'Mind what you say, and say the kettle is left out every night'. George Green, her son, was called to give evidence and his mother cautioned him with the words, 'Mind what you say, and say that we were all sick down the yard'.

The Police Constable ended his damning deposition by telling the court that he had observed Mrs Green returning to the kitchen after having given her evidence to the inquest. She had allegedly said, 'they make me laugh even though I am only half-well'. At this point, the newspaper recorded that Mrs Green had claimed this was just a story.

Mr Dyer pursued the matter with PC Raynor, who elaborated on his deposition by saying that Mrs Green had burst out laughing and that this had been witnessed by Mrs Stringer, Mrs Stopper, Mrs Rowson, George Green and others, who were in the kitchen at the time.

Colonel Moore recalled Mrs Stopper, who said that her sister did not laugh or say anything about being not half-well; on the contrary, she was crying. Her story was also checked by Mr Bean, with Mrs

Stopper adding that she was looking directly at Mrs Green when she came out of the room. Mrs Rowson was also recalled, but she was a little less definite, if not evasive: she had not seen or heard Mrs Green laughing; she remembered her coming out of the room, but was not taking a great deal of notice.

Ann Stringer, a Boston nurse, had been at the inquest, although she did not give evidence before the adjournment. She recalled seeing George Green going in to give his evidence and hearing his mother say to him, 'Speak the truth – you know you have seen the kettle there scores of times; and you say so'. She also said to him, 'You say that we were all three sick down the yard'. Further, she had heard Mrs Green say to her sister, Mrs Stopper, before going in to give evidence, 'You can say that you have seen the kettle there scores of times'.

Mrs Stringer continued her deposition by recalling a visit to the house of Mrs and Mrs Green on the 17th May. At this point, she referred to a dress which had obviously been presented in court as evidence at the time. The reader is left by the newspaper to work out the exact significance of the dress from what Mrs Stringer told the court. She deposed that on the day that Thomas Green died, his wife was wearing the dress, as she had pulled a handkerchief out of its pocket. The pocket of the dress, now in front of Mrs Stringer, had been cut out and was confirmed by the holes: Mrs Green had used the pocket regularly, up to her wearing mourning.

Finally, she confirmed that she was in the kitchen at the inquest, standing by the door, but did not notice Mrs Green come out from giving her evidence.

The next three witnesses to depose did not have a great deal to say individually, but cumulatively, following on from each other in close proximity, they created a strong sense of Ellen Green having a flagrant disregard for the constraints of social respectability.

Elizabeth Wood, the wife of John Wood, who was the foreman of Edward Porter at Frith Bank Farm, deposed that she had invited Ellen Green to come and spend a few days with her. She had arrived at the time of the New Year Market, accompanied by John Bonnett, but not her husband. They stayed all night and left in the afternoon. Mrs Wood had not been surprised that they came together. Questioned by Mr Bailes, Mrs Wood said that she had invited Thomas Green to come with them; she had also invited John Bonnett at Christmas.

John Mitchell, a labourer, resident in Boston, knew Ellen Green and John Bonnett by sight. On the last Saturday of April, he had shared a railway compartment with them on his way to Lincoln. He had seen the couple that night in a booth together: if the husband was there, he was not aware of it. Questioned by Mr Bailes, John Mitchell was able to say that there was another woman with them; the version of the reply in the *Boston Guardian and Independent* was slightly different and more precise: he said that he did not know that Mrs Rowson was with them at the time.

The Fishtoft gardener, William Yates, claimed to know Mrs and Mrs Green very well, having lived quite close to them for over two years. He also knew John Bonnett. Mr Yates deposed that he had seen Ellen Green and John Bonnett together at Boston market on a Saturday night, as well as standing together at the gate. The well-informed Mr Yates had heard Mrs and Mrs Green arguing with each other as he walked past the house, probably on about half a dozen occasions.

Mr Dyer pressed the witness concerning the precise dates on which he had heard them quarrelling, but he was unable to help him.

In the version of the deposition by Mr Yates published in the *Boston Guardian and Lincolnshire Independent*, his dislike of Mrs Green was even more evident: he had forbidden his wife to go and see Mrs Green and told the court that when he overheard the heated words between husband and wife, 'she appeared to be in the most quarrelsome mood'.

The hearing moved on from the anecdotal tittle-tattle of the unofficial neighbourhood watch to the more solid factual world of Superintendent Thoresby, who at around 5.30 on the 13th May, had assisted in a search of the house. In a brief exchange with Mrs Green, who was lying on her couch at the time, she told him that she had been poisoned by somebody having put something into the kettle which she had left outside. Superintendent Thoresby, at the invitation of Mrs Green, had searched the house for evidence of poison, but had found nothing. He decided to remove various objects: the sugar basin which was on the table and the tea caddy and tea kettle which were in the back-house. In passing, he mentioned that Mrs Green was wearing the dress which had been shown in court, but without elaborating on his observation.

The superintendent returned on the 20th May to conduct a more thorough search of the premises. On this occasion, he and his men were more successful in their search for evidence, having found a quantity of white powder amongst the ashes outside, which he carefully placed in a canister. An investigation of the petty-hole revealed a white power adhering to the front of the seat, which had been thrown from right to left. A removal of a large flag stone also produced a further quantity of white powder. The various samples were put together, parcelled up and removed.

Superintendent Thoresby concluded his deposition with an impressive list of evidence which he had taken to Dr G M Lowe, the County Analyst, on the 10th June. The amassed evidence included: a tea-pot given to him by Dr Arthur Tuxford on the

13th of May; two jars of viscera and a bottle of water given to him by Dr James Tuxford on the 17th of May; separate parcels containing ashes, tea, sugar from both the basin and the cupboard; a jar containing the vomit of George Green; a canister containing white powder from the ashes; and a number fragments of soiled pieces of paper from the vault of the petty-hole.

The superintendent had certainly been diligent in his search and retrieve operation: Dr Lowe must have been delighted.

On the 19th May, he had apprehended Mrs Green with a warrant for her arrest, which was read out to her: the prisoner had made no reply.

The next day, Superintendent Thoresby returned to the house and examined the dress worn by Mrs Green, which he found to have had the pocket recently cut out, but once again, he did not elaborate on the significance of his discovery.

The final witness was Dr George May Lowe, who had taken possession of the evidence from Superintendent Thoresby, in his office at Number 2, Cornhill, Lincoln. The meticulous analyst read out to the court the list of eleven items which he had received, sealed and labelled, and then went through them, one by one, with his conclusions. He had discovered arsenic in most of the items given to him by the superintendent: the only exceptions were item 5, a tea caddy containing half an ounce of tea leaves;

item 6, a packet of sugar; item 7, another packet containing sugar; item 8, a yellow jar containing the vomit of George Green; and item 10, a small bottle containing sodium carbonate.

On the 24th May, Dr Lowe had also received a parcel of sugar from Dr Edward Tuxford, which did not contain any poisonous substance.

He concluded that boiled water would take up to twelve grains of arsenic to the fluid ounce and that a large cup would contain sufficient to destroy life.

The conclusion of the proceedings was oddly anticlimactic. Mr Bean said that he intended to leave the verdict in the capable hands of the Bench and Mr Bailes simply stated there had been no evidence to link John Bonnett with the crime and he should therefore be discharged. Mr Dyer was more loquacious in defence of Mrs Green: whilst not intending to review the voluminous depositions, he insisted that there was no real evidence to prove the guilt of his client. The leaving of a kettle outside was a circumstance which was not unusual; her laughing on coming out of the Coroner's jury room, the cutting of the pocket from the dress and the statements made by her, were insufficient to commit her to trial.

In an unexpected turn of events, Mr Dyer wanted to recall Mrs Stopper, but the Bench refused the request. The *Lincolnshire Chronicle* gave the reader no explanation for Mr Dyer's belated request, but the matter was clarified by the Boston newspaper. Mr Dyer told the court that it was Mrs Stopper who had taken the pocket from the dress, in order to wash it, and that recalling her would prove it.

The Bench retired, returned and discharged John Bonnett; Mrs Green, despite the pleas of Mr Dyer, was sent for trial at Lincoln. Bail was applied for, but refused.

Trial Of Ellen Green For Wilful Murder, At The Lincoln Assizes, Monday, 25th July, 1875

The Summer Assizes commenced on Thursday, 21st July, with the arrival in Lincoln of the newly created Justice of the Court of Common Pleas, Mr Nathaniel Lindley, accompanied by Mr Justice Field. Justice Lindley was to preside over the business of the Crown Court, whilst Justice Field took charge of the Nisi Prius Court.

The Grand Jury consisted of the following:
- Honourable Murray Edward Gordon Finch-Hatton (Foreman)
- Samuel Allenby
- Richard C Bergne-Coupland
- Max H Dallison
- Richard George Ellison
- William Robert Emeris

- John Ferraby
- Richard Gleed
- Frederick Lyon Hopkins
- William Hutton
- George Augustus Luard
- Charles Massingberd-Mundy
- Colonel Charles Thomas John Moore
- George Neville
- Edward Peacock
- Meaburn Staniland
- Robert John Taylor
- Arthur Trollope
- John Earle Welby
- Samuel Wright Wright

The list of cases on the Calendar for the Grand Jury to consider was dismal and depressing, including a Boston doctor charged with the criminal negligence of a patient, leading to her death, child murder by a servant at Pinchbeck and the alleged killing of a grocer's assistant in Boston.

The two most serious and difficult cases also involved wilful murder. Peter Blanchard, an epilepsy sufferer and persistent bed-wetter, stood accused of killing Louisa Hodgson at Louth, although the Grand Jury was not required to discuss the case immediately, as a true bill had already been found against Blanchard in a previous Assize session. The trial of Blanchard was to take up most of the day's business at the Crown Court, on Friday 23rd May, ending with him being sentenced to death by Justice Lindley, after the unfortunate man had delivered a moving speech to the court advising the world to learn from his sorry example.

In his opening remarks on the Calendar, Judge Lindley drew the attention of the Grand Jury to the case of Ellen Green, who stood indicted of murdering her husband by poison. Outlining the circumstances of the case, he drew particular attention to the prosecution having alleged that Mrs Green 'for some reason' had put arsenic in a kettle, which led to the poisoning of her husband and her son, although the latter had survived and would be giving evidence.

The trial of Ellen Green, in front of Justice Lindley, starting at 10 o'clock on Monday, 25th July, was to last all day, including a deliberation of nearly two hours by the jury. Both the time required by the jury to reach a decision, as well as the judicial fate of Peter Blanchard a couple of days earlier, may have caused some concern to Ellen Green and her supporters, as they awaited the verdict later that day.

Anticipating high drama, the public space in court was 'crowded in every part': it was an interest reflected in an equally packed report published in the *Lincolnshire Chronicle*, on the 30th July, which extended over four columns of dense small print.

The two Counsels contending the issues were both experienced and formidable opponents: Mr James Fitzjames Stephen, who had successfully defended Elizabeth Dodds in 1860, was the Counsel for the Prosecution; Mr John Compton Lawrance, who had attempted, but ultimately failed, to defend the difficult case of Priscilla Biggadike in 1868, acted as Counsel for the Defence.

The sheer number of witness statements of varying degrees of reliability, most of which were already in the public domain by way of the existing newspaper reports on the hearing at the Sessions House, produced very obvious reporting difficulties in terms of informing the public, whilst avoiding too much repetition.

One solution was to report fully on the words of both Counsels as they tried to persuade the Grand Jury of the guilt or innocence of the prisoner. The newspaper could now also include the testimony of John Bonnett, the alleged paramour of Ellen Green, who had been acquitted in Boston of any wrongdoing.

The report in the *Lincolnshire Chronicle* described Mrs Green as a 'short, thick-set woman, with a remarkably dark complexion, heightened by the black bonnet and dress she wore'. When asked, she pleaded Not Guilty, 'in a barely audible voice'.

The image of Mrs Green, according to the report, shifted dramatically as the trial progressed. At first, she appeared to be calm and collected, but she gradually became 'more excited', and before the case for the Prosecution was finished, she was 'weeping copiously' and rocked herself on the chair on which she was sitting. Mrs Green appeared to become even more distressed during the closing speech of the Counsel for the Defence, when she 'sobbed loudly', hiding her face behind her handkerchief when her dead husband and her still living son were mentioned. The report made no comment upon Mrs Green's behaviour, leaving it for the reader to judge whether it was the intolerable anguish of a woman whose life was under threat, or the cynical theatricality of a wife who, having dispatched her husband with arsenic was trying to manipulate a jury.

What it did comment upon was the behaviour of some people in the public gallery whose 'ill-timed levity' during the trial had to be censured by Justice Lindley.

It may be, of course, that the melodramatic description of Mrs Green in court was staged by the reporter, rather than enacted by the prisoner. The account of Mrs Green's behaviour by the *Nottingham Guardian*'s reporter, for example, created a quite different, more unruffled image. Up to the close of the trial, she had 'remained apparently indifferent to, and unconscious of, her awful position'. During the serious disclosures which were being made against her 'she kept her lips compressed', and it was only at the conclusion of the case for the Prosecution, that she seemed to realise the full enormity of her situation. However, she soon resumed her former composure which she maintained until the jury returned a verdict in her favour.

Mr Stephen opened the case for the Prosecution by alerting the jury to the issues facing them. The case was not a straightforward one of dealing with simple facts, but a more taxing one of piecing together a series of circumstances which taken individually might appear 'trifling and unimportant', but seen as a whole, became very significant.

The Counsel proceeded to identify the key facts of the matter, which in his opinion the Counsel for the Defence would acknowledge as true, but from which he would draw different inferences. First, even though the prisoner herself had drunk some tea on the day in question, she was not made seriously ill, compared to her husband and son. Secondly, according to the medical evidence, the amount of arsenic required to kill someone was only three grains, but the body of the deceased had contained twenty-four grains. There were only three options for the jury to consider: the deceased either killed himself, was murdered by his wife or by someone who had attempted to murder the whole family.

He then drew attention to the numerous and often

contradictory statements made by the prisoner both before and after the death of her husband, and invited the jury to consider their truthfulness. At first, she had tried to blame some unknown person, but then had switched her story when a quantity of arsenic had been found in the house, in places where it was not customary to store it. In order to draw attention away from herself, she then invented a confession of suicide by her husband. Could the jury believe such a story, he asked, when he could have told the same story to the magistrate in his dying declaration and in the process have absolved his wife from any 'horrible imputation'? Further, if she knew this to be the truth of the matter, wouldn't she have let other people know, in order to get her husband to admit it? In a tone of mocking incredulity, Mr Stephens pointed out to the jury that Mrs Green had waited a whole fortnight before telling anyone 'the grand secret'.

He concluded his opening remarks by suggesting that Mrs Green had a motive for poisoning her husband and that arose from her intimacy with the John Bonnett, who had asked her to elope with him and to whom she had expressed a wish to be single.

The first deposition reported was from George Green, mistakenly given the wrong name of Joseph. His account repeated his recollections of the morning of Thursday, the 13th May, heard at the inquest and the hearing, which focused upon the drinking of tea by the different members of the family. The only significant addition was that the tea had been poured out into Thomas Green's cup before he had arrived at the breakfast table, thus the boy did not see it being poured out . He also recalled the effect of the arsenic on his father and mother, as well as on himself. All three were sick in the yard, although his father was much worse than his mother.

Dr Tuxford had arrived at about 8.45: at that point, his father was in bed and he was in bed, but he didn't know the whereabouts of his mother.

The final part of his deposition referred to his giving evidence at the inquest: his mother had told him to tell the truth, but she did not mention a kettle.

Under questioning by Mr Lawrance, George Green provided useful material for the Counsel in his later summing up of the case. He confirmed that there had been nothing different about the breakfast arrangements on the morning of the 13th May. He also confirmed that he knew his aunt, Mrs Stopper, was coming to breakfast, but she had not arrived on time; further, that he also knew that Mr Moore, the greengrocer, was expected at breakfast too, having arranged to help his father to cut some cabbages.

George Green had slept in the same room as his father during his illness and was with him when he died. His mother did not sleep in the same bedroom, but she was also with him when he died. The boy ended his reply to Mr Lawrance by repeating the story of the words of love spoken by between his mother and father, adding that his mother was in the habit of leaving the kettle outside by the pump.

The boy was re-examined by Mr Stephen in order to get greater clarity concerning the conversation between his parents in his father's dying hours. Unfortunately, he was not able to hear what had been said, as his father spoke very quietly. He also added that a number of people were in the room during his illness and that he had spent three days in the bedroom.

Sarah Stopper's deposition was the same as that heard at the inquest and the Boston hearing, relating to her discovery of the family in the yard. Questioned by Mr Lawrance, she told the court that she was at the house all day, looking after her brother-in-law and nephew, whilst her sister lay ill on the sofa. Dr Tuxford had attended four times on the 13th May and had given them all some medicine, although the report does not make it clear which Dr Tuxford she meant.

In response to the probing of the Counsel for the Prosecution, Mrs Stopper appeared to give an account of her sister being sick which was slightly different from anything reported earlier in terms of the frequency of her vomiting. She had seen her sister being sick twice in the yard and also during the day, more often in the afternoon than in the morning. In her opinion, her sister was sick as much before being attended by Dr Arthur Tuxford, as afterwards: it was clear that Mr Stephen was trying to establish the idea of Mrs Green being sick having been caused by an emetic rather than arsenic poisoning.

The deposition of Mrs Rowson was an interesting one in that it referred to her alleged presence in the bedroom of Thomas Green, along with Mrs Allen, their having been asked to leave just before confessing his suicide to his wife. It started with a repetition of her deposition at the hearing, with the addition that she had gone home before the doctor had arrived at the house and returned several times during the course of the day. She also deposed that Mrs Green had been sick before the arrival of Dr Arthur Tuxford.

Mrs Rowson had been in and out of the house during the days of Thomas Green's illness and death. She confirmed the story of Mrs Green that she had been in the bedroom with Mrs Allen on the Saturday. However, Thomas Green had not told her or Mrs Allen to leave the room, as had been claimed by Ellen Green. Rather, she had heard him say 'Close the door' to her husband and John Allen who were both in the room at the time, as Thomas Green was about to make his will: she was not in the room when she heard this.

Mrs Rowson had earlier given evidence related

to a trip to Lincoln involving Mrs Green and John Bonnett: she did so again, although the latest version included a statement that the prisoner and Bonnett had not sat together in the railway carriage on the way to Lincoln. She also mentioned that in Lincoln she had gone to buy refreshments and had been accompanied by Mrs Green and Bonnett, which was a slightly different version from her earlier deposition which had mentioned going into a dancing room. John Bonnett, she told the court, used to lodge with her. A similarly anodyne version of the trip to Skegness was repeated which involved seeing Mrs Green with Bonnett and another young man. She repeated her evidence, however, that she did not see Thomas Green at either Lincoln or Skegness.

Mr Lawrance was clearly interested in the evidence relating to what had happened on the Saturday morning when his client had rather dubiously, according to the Prosecution, heard a confession of suicide. Under questioning, Esmeranda Rowson, introduced further important clarifications, as well as an individual not hitherto mentioned. She told the court that Mrs Green was in the bedroom at the same time as her husband and Mr Allen; and further, the village schoolmaster, Mr Soar, was also present, having been fetched to assist with something connected with the will, although she did not know whether a will was made. There was no mention of the supposed suicide confession, but Mrs Rowson did helpfully say that Thomas Green had given his wife permission to go to Lincoln; less helpfully, she wasn't sure whether Ellen Green had taken medicine before she was sick.

Dr James Tuxford described being called out and finding Mr Green 'in a state of great prostration, complaining of a burning sensation in his throat and stomach, and very sick'. The boy was the same, but not so prostrate, but Mrs Green showed none of the same symptoms. What he did say, and repeated, was that she seemed 'very depressed in her mind'. Dr Tuxford was very clear that the condition of the father and son was very different from that of the mother. The father had 'endured excessive cramps and sweating' until he died; the boy had suffered from excessive vomiting until he recovered after three days; the mother had said that she had been sick in the afternoon of the first day, but after that made no complaint about her health. He had given emetics to the father and the boy, but not to the mother, as she did not require treatment: he mentioned, perhaps somewhat sceptically, that Mrs Green 'was always lying on the sofa'.

Mr Lawrance pressed the doctor on whether or not his son, Arthur Tuxford, had given Mrs Green some medicine. He believed that this had been the case, but insisted that there had been no symptoms of arsenic poison, only a sense that she was 'depressed in mind'. He also repeated his observation that Mrs Green 'was on the sofa every time I went to the house'.

The final time he had attended Thomas Green was on the Sunday before he died; Arthur Tuxford had seen him later, before he had died on the Monday morning of 'exhaustion from the poisoning'.

The deposition of Dr Arthur Tuxford corroborated that of his father, including the new evidence that Mrs Green appeared to be suffering from being 'troubled in her mind'. She had complained of being in great pain and had given her medicine on the Thursday only, which might have made her sick. He had been back to the house on the Sunday and she was walking about, without making any complaints about her health.

Dr George Lowe was the expert witness as far as the medical evidence was concerned. After going through the various pieces of evidence described in Boston, which he had received from Superintendent Thoresby, he went into greater detail concerning the impact of arsenic in solution on the human body. He began by stating that in the bottle of water he had analysed, he had found five grains of arsenic to the fluid ounce of water. Further, he deposed that arsenic dissolved much more quickly in hot water than in cold and that should it be boiled for an hour, it would take up to twelve grains of arsenic to the fluid ounce of hot water; therefore, if boiled for just half an hour, it would take up to six grains of arsenic. The four small tea cups he examined would have contained four fluid ounces of water, the larger one, used by Thomas Green, would have contained eight fluid ounces. A person drinking a small cupful would ingest twenty grains of arsenic, whilst a person drinking from the larger cup would ingest forty grains: it only took two or three grains to kill an adult. Anyone drinking a small cupful would be unlikely to survive. Perhaps more significant for the Prosecution was that anyone drinking a teacup containing ten grains of arsenic could not have recovered by the following day. Any competent medical man would recognise the symptoms of arsenical poisoning within two days of a person consuming ten grains of arsenic. Even more telling, immediate vomiting would not remove the symptoms of arsenic poison.

Mr Lawrance, no doubt, recognised the weight of medical evidence being against Mrs Green, and would have found it difficult to challenge the expertise of Dr Lowe. He therefore queried the uniformity of individual reactions to arsenic poisoning: Dr Lowe told the court that the length of time before symptoms became evident as well as their severity differed from person to person. Mr Stephen followed a different line of questioning by presenting Dr Lowe with a hypothetical question: if a person vomited once after ingesting ten grains of arsenic and there was no medical intervention for five hours, would he expect to observe nothing more than a pain in the stomach? The doctor confirmed that in such a situation he would expect more serious symptoms than a pain in the stomach.

John Thomas Moore, the Boston greengrocer, who had presented evidence in Boston which suggested that Thomas Green was sure that he had been deliberately poisoned repeated his testimony. He also added that whilst he was in the deceased's bedroom with him, he had vomited ten or twelve times into a basin, which he held for him: Mr Green, in contrast to his wife, was clearly a very ill man. He also changed his deposition slightly, by claiming that he was in the house for about an hour, as opposed to half an hour, and that he returned every day to check on the health of Thomas Green. On each visit, the prisoner had been in the room.

Moore confirmed that Mrs Green had explained in detail what had happened that morning, including her realisation that the tea had been poisoned and an insistence that the kettle had been left out all night.

He was questioned by the Counsel for the Defence, who had asked him how long he had known the Greens and whether they lived in domestic harmony, as far as he knew. He told the court that he had known them for three years, that he was a frequent visitor to the house and that he was not aware of any marital difficulties, just as had done at Boston. He also said that he was in the room when Thomas Green had died and that he had been insensible and very weak.

The deposition from John Ostler, as reported by the *Lincolnshire Chronicle*, varied little from that heard in Boston, although he did shift his testimony slightly when he said that he did not hear Mrs Green's reply to Sergeant Henson's question to her about the cause of the family's illness.

Elizabeth Ostler retold the same story of her conversations and visits to the Green house, with no variation. She was cross-examined by Mr Lawrance and told the court that Thomas Green had died at about 8.30 in the morning, and that the last time she had seen him alive was at 5.30.

Frederick Swain, the friend of Thomas Green, who had allegedly witnessed the unpleasant exchange between man and wife just a few hours before his death was also sticking to his story. Mr Lawrance, like Mr Dyer at the Boston hearing, probed Frederick Swain's account: like Mr Dyer, he was keen to establish that the brother and sister of Thomas Green were in the room when the exchange took place. In addition, he ascertained from the witness that he was in the house for only half-an-hour and that Thomas Green, when he saw him, was weak and suffering great pain. Frederick Swain also repeated his story about having seen Mrs Green and John Bonnett together at the Boston Fair, but neither the Prosecution nor the Defence Counsels pressed him on his story.

Sergeant Henson had given a very comprehensive account of his dealings with Mrs Green in front of the Boston magistrates, including the alleged suicide confession, which he repeated to the court. An interesting and very precise addition, mentioned almost in passing, was that the colour of Battle's mouse poisoning was blue. The reference to the Lincoln chemist J W Battle was in the context of Mrs Green's observation that the poison thrown away by her husband was white: in short, arsenic rather than *Battle's Vermin Killer*, whose deadly ingredient was strychnine.

Mr Lawrance cross-examined the police officer, whose only recorded response was to confirm that Mrs Green had insisted that someone had put arsenic in the kettle or the pump nozzle: given the frequency of the claim made by Mrs Green to various people, that the kettle or the pump was the source of the poison, it seemed a rather redundant repetition.

Police Constable Isaac Raynor (now renamed Rider) seemed to have been a witness of greater interest to both Counsels, as well as to the judge himself, possibly because he had presented evidence in Boston which suggested that Ellen Green had attempted to prime witnesses before they gave evidence and therefore pervert the course of justice. The constable repeated his evidence concerning what Mrs Green had said to her sister and son, word for word: unfortunately for the police constable, his precise words shifted under cross-examination by Mr Lawrance. Either because of the pressure of the moment or because he had not made a written note of them, he changed the words of Ellen Green to Mrs Stopper from '*Mind what you say*, and say the kettle is left out every night' to '*Speak the truth*, and say that the kettle is left out every night'. The police constable, if the report is accurate, seemed to become uncomfortable at this point, following it up with the defensive assertion, 'That is what I meant when I said she said 'Mind what you say''. The Counsel for the Defence knew that he was on the point of undermining the reliability of a key witness: in a tersely dismissive question he asked the police officer, 'You think they are the same do you?' to which the naïve or mistaken constable replied, 'Yes'. The final words of Mr Lawrance on hearing the response of the constable resembled a headmaster dismissing a naughty schoolboy from his study: 'Then you may go'.

The issue of who said what in the kitchen of Mr Allen became even more confused as Mr Stephen and the Judge attempted to establish some kind of clarity. In response to Mr Stephen's cross-examination, the constable seemed to change his story back to his original deposition, asserting 'I did not hear her say 'Speak the truth', but I heard her say 'Mind what you say''. In reply to a question from Justice Lindley, the constable was certain that what he reported Mrs Green saying to George Green was accurate, but he had not recorded it in his notebook.

In a further attempt to clear up the ambiguity, his Lordship recalled George Green, who said that his mother had told him to say that they had all been sick down the yard. The lack of any ambiguity in the young boy's statement seemed to offer hope of at least a partial resolution. Unfortunately, and not for the first time, George Green blurred the issue: under cross-examination from Mr Stephen, he stated that his mother had told him, 'Mind what you say'; but she had also said, 'Speak the truth''.

The jury may well have been baffled at this point.

However, all was not lost, as the police constable had told the hearing in Boston that there were two independent witnesses in the kitchen who might vouch for the accuracy of his deposition: Ann Stringer and Esmeranda Rowson.

Ann Stringer was called, but Mrs Rowson was not. In her deposition in Boston, Mrs Stringer claimed that she had heard Ellen Green say to her sister, 'You can say that you have seen the kettle there scores of times'. Omitting the word 'can', Mrs Stringer gave the same evidence to the court. Her memories of the conversation between George Green and his mother diverged more significantly, however. At Boston, she had deposed that she heard the prisoner say, 'Speak the truth – you know you have seen the kettle there scores of times, and you say so'; and also, 'You say that we were all three sick down the yard'. Her latest version of the conversation in the kitchen was one in which George Green was an active participant in the conversation. His mother had said to him, 'Speak the truth, and say that we were all sick down the yard. Say that you've seen the kettle there scores of times'. According to Mrs Stringer, George replied. 'No, I didn't get home last night, and I don't know'.

The jury may well have continued to feel even more baffled.

Elizabeth Wood, a mutual friend of Ellen Green and of John Bonnett, had supplied evidence at the Boston hearing of the two having spent New Year's Eve together at her house. Mrs Wood re-told the story, except this time adding details which made the story less scurrilous. Both she and Mrs Green had gone to bed at around two o'clock in the morning and John Bonnett had spent the night in a bedroom at the back of the house. They left the house together the following afternoon.

The testimonies of John Mitchell and William Yates, based mainly on inconclusive anecdote, differed very little to the versions heard in Boston, and their answers under cross-examination did little to clarify or extend their original depositions.

The calling of John Bonnett, waggoner, to the witness stand, however, was potentially a defining moment in the case. He had been linked to the life of Mrs Green by a number of witnesses, including Mrs Green herself, but remained a somewhat elusive figure in the various depositions. His testimony, under cross-examination by Mr Stephen, unfortunately, was an embarrassing and unhelpful mixture of coarse buffoonery and a seeming total lack of awareness that Mrs Green might be facing a death sentence.

Mr Bonnett informed the court that Ellen Green had told him more than once that she wished that she was single. He had thought that it was a joke, 'as I have a good many more'. Perhaps sensing a further opportunity to entertain the courtroom with stories of his amorous exploits, as well as enhance his reputation as a bit of a card, he then asserted, 'I never took liberties with her, not that I am aware of'. The Fishtoft lothario was clearly on a roll, as he assured the jury that, 'I have never told anybody that I have romped and played with her'.

Unfortunately for Mr Bonnett, that was his final word on the subject, as an unappreciative Mr Lawrance brought the curtain down on his braggadocio performance by objecting to the testimony: with that, John Bonnett was sent packing from the witness box.

The reason for the objection to the testimony of a key witness was not easy to work out, other than its obviously offensive and indelicate language in a court of law. However, the real reason was apparently a more formal one, explained by the *Leicester Daily Post*: no notice that John Bonnett's was going to be called had been given to Mr Lawrance and Mr Stephen had proposed to treat him as a hostile witness: Justice Lindley ruled that he could not do so, and so the rumbustious performance of Mr Bonnett was never mentioned again.

The solid and reliable testimony of Superintendent Thoresby, describing his search for arsenic in Mrs Green's house, would no doubt have been a relief to Mr Lawrance after the improprieties of John Bonnett's uncouth display, although perhaps an anti-climax to the public gallery in need of a respite from the tedium of dry details and bewildering contradictory depositions.

Superintendent Thoresby produced nothing new in his deposition, other than telling the court that he had read the arrest warrant to Mrs Green, but she had made no answer.

The dying declaration of Thomas Green, which his wife had allegedly objected to being heard without her input and which Mrs Stopper had done her best to hear through the bedroom door, would perhaps have been expected to clinch the case one way or the other: it had the reliability of being heard and proven by a police officer, a magistrate and his clerk, and was a first-hand account from the victim of the crime.

It was now being heard for the first time in public, but was a disappointment in terms of taking the case forward and helping the jury. It amounted to a narrative which was already in the public domain of a man being poisoned by a cup of breakfast tea, along with his wife and son, and that he was very ill. There was nothing in the final deposition of Thomas Green which was useful to the Prosecution; the case for the Defence, however, possibly benefited from the statement that Mrs Stopper was expected for breakfast that morning and that both his wife and his son had been sick in the yard. Tantalisingly, or frustratingly, Mr Green deposed that the kettle was usually left outside against the pump, but he could not say for certain that it was there on the Wednesday night.

Dr Walter Clegg, the Coroner at the inquest, was the next witness to be called: he repeated the statement which Mrs Green had made to him under oath, and most of his deposition consisted of several reassurances that he had warned the prisoner against providing evidence which could be used against her.

The final witness to be called was Lucy Allen, who had attended Mr Green up to the time of his death. Her deposition had a sense of an afterthought in that it merely consisted of a statement that she had never been asked to leave the deceased's bedroom just before his supposed confession of suicide, as had been claimed by Ellen Green.

In his summing up to the court, Mr Stephen built his case against the prisoner mainly on the strength of the measurable difference between the condition of her husband and son after drinking the poisoned tea, and that of Mrs Green herself. It may be, he suggested, that George Green had not observed the quantity of tea consumed by his mother correctly, but it was a remarkable fact that whilst the boy had drunk roughly the same amount as his mother, he was ill for three days and in danger of losing his life, whilst she was not ill at all: something which the medical men had all agreed upon. It was clear, as far as the Prosecution was concerned, that the prisoner could not possibly have drunk the same amount of tea and therefore ingested the same amount of arsenic as her son.

Mr Stephen moved on to the various statements which Ellen Green has made during the course of the investigation. In particular, he drew the attention of the jury to the supposed confession of Thomas Green to his wife that he had put arsenic in the kettle. Mr Stephen strongly suggested that such a confession, involving not only the destruction of himself, but also of his wife and child, was totally improbable. Further, whilst the inconsistent suggestion from Mrs Green that it was John Bonnett, was equally improbable, that claim not only showed a connection between the two, but also pointed to the prisoner's misconduct and her inconsistent story telling.

Mr Lawrance spoke at length in defence of Ellen Green, claiming that there was not a shred of evidence to prove that she had either put poison in the kettle or was aware of the presence of arsenic in the tea as she poured it. Whilst he admitted, in a spirit of reasonableness, that the jury might entertain doubts and suspicions about the guilt of the prisoner, it could not convict Mrs Green on mere doubts and suspicions, but on clear evidence alone.

The two main points which Mr Lawrance wished the jury to consider were the fact that Mrs Green also drank the poisoned tea and that other people had been invited to breakfast that morning, both of which, he asserted, 'were explosive of the theory of the Prosecution'.

The *Lincolnshire Chronicle* expended a considerable amount of column inches on the two summary statements, but the reader is left with a sense of a good deal of material having been omitted. The trial had involved nearly twenty witnesses, a number of significant contradictions and a great deal of ambiguity surrounding the words and actions of the prisoner. After a trial lasting all day, requiring more subtle arguments than the ones presented in the report, the generalised account, especially of the Defence case, was ultimately unhelpful for a well-informed understanding of the final verdict of Not Guilty.

The reader may have been hoping for more helpful detail from the report of the summing up by Justice Lindley, but would have been left disappointed. His Lordship had reviewed the evidence and had impartially cast doubts on both sides of the case, most notably, the improbability of Mrs Green having put poison in the tea and the improbability of Mr Green having done it himself. In the final analysis, the newspaper was satisfied with informing the reader that the judge had 'carefully dwelt on the contradictory statements of the prisoner and all the other salient features of the case, both for the Prosecution and the Defence'.

The difficulties of the case were perhaps more effectively summed by the report that the jury retired at 5.50 and only reached its decision of Not Guilty after nearly two hours of discussion.

The *Stamford Mercury* of the 30th July also reported on the trial, but in a much shorter version, which summarised the progress of proceedings, rather than reporting upon the contributions of individual witnesses and any cross-examinations which took place.

However, the Stamford newspaper did report in greater detail on the closing statement by Mr Lawrance and in so doing, filled in many of the gaps left by the *Lincolnshire Chronicle*. In passing, it also provided a better understanding of the various positions taken up by the Prosecution Counsel, which he was challenging.

Mr Lawrance made great play of the fact that several people were arriving at the house the day of the poisoning to eat breakfast: Mrs Stopper, Mr Moore and also George Green, who had been away from home for the week, were due to eat with Mr and Mrs Green that morning. In Mr Lawrance's opinion, if Mrs Green was planning to kill her husband, 'it was about the last morning of all mornings that she would have chosen'.

The Counsel for the Prosecution had suggested that Mrs Green either did not drink any tea, had 'shammed' drinking tea or had drunk only the smallest amount. Mr Lawrance strongly refuted all three of these possibilities. First, it had been testified by several witnesses that Mrs Green had been sick after drinking the tea, including her son, the doctor who had given her medicine and, most telling of all, 'the voice from beyond the grave', in the dying deposition of Thomas Green. Secondly, the suggestion from the Prosecution that Mrs Green had taken a drink of poisoned tea 'blind', having no expertise on the impact of particular quantities of arsenic on the human body and so endangering her own life, was beyond belief.

Mrs Green's insistence that the kettle had been left out all night and that it was customary for her to leave it there was also supported by the statements of her son and also her husband, in his dying deposition, and that it had been left out on the night of the 16th May. If the reporting of the speech by Mr Lawrance is accurate, the Counsel for the Defence was either not remembering correctly or was being deliberately misleading. George Green had confirmed that his mother left the kettle out all night, but he could not say that he had seen it outside on the night of Wednesday, 12th May, as he was away from home at the time. Further, according to the version of Thomas Green's deposition printed in the *Lincolnshire Chronicle*, he was unable to say that he had seen the kettle outside that night. That Mr Lawrance, as opposed to the newspaper, had got the wrong date, might have undermined his reliability at this point.

Mr Lawrance was also at great pains to make it clear to the jury that whilst there had been a connection between Mrs Green and John Bonnett, there was no evidence to suggest impropriety; quite the opposite – Mr and Mrs Green had lived 'on affectionate terms'. It was no great surprise that the Learned Counsel made no reference to John Bonnett's denial of 'romping' and 'playing' with Mrs Green to support his case.

In response to the Prosecution having pointed out the contradictory nature of Mrs Green's statements, Mr Lawrance took the bull by the horns, and admitted that there were inconsistencies in what Mrs Green had told them. However, in a final rhetorical flourish, he addressed the jury directly: 'surely they were not going to say because the woman told a lie, they were satisfied that she had poisoned her husband'. As a legal nicety it was correct; as a sound moral position, it was perhaps rather dubious in its implications.

The *Grantham Journal* of the 31st July, took little interest in the case, reporting the trial in around twenty lines. The *Sleaford Gazette* showed even less interest, although it did triumphantly report its discovery that Mrs Green was the aunt of Matilda Barber of Pinchbeck, who at the same Assize session had been tried for cutting the throat of her infant son with a pen-knife.

Unfortunately for the newspaper, the sensational scoop was almost certainly a total fabrication, based upon the fleeting mention of a Mrs Green at the trial of Matilda Barber, and who had nursed her during the course of her troubles.

In all probability, Mrs Green managed to get back home safely to Fishtoft the day after her acquittal, without any further harassment.

However, it was not the end of her short but

inglorious life in the public spotlight, at least as far as the popular press was concerned.

On the 25th of September, just eight weeks after the acquittal, the *Boston Guardian* published a short article titled 'The Widow Green'. Its position, between a congratulatory story celebrating the Cheavins Filter Works in Boston having won a silver medal, awarded by the Northamptonshire Agricultural Society, and a notice relating to a pay out by the Shipwrecked Mariners' Society to the widow of Joseph Nightingale, a deceased master-mariner, seemed somewhat incongruous in view of its subject matter. After briefly reminding the reader of the background to the Fishtoft murder trial, the astonishing article recorded the marriage of Ellen Green and John Bonnett at Horncastle. The brazen indelicacy of the marriage took some believing and indeed, it was not meant to be believed, as the notice ended with a piece of journalistic gallows humour. The choice of Horncastle as the place for the happy couple to get married was an invention to create the opportunity for a grim joke which referenced William Marwood, the town's cobbler and public executioner: 'Marwood did not 'tie the knot' though doubtless he would have been glad enough to do so'.

The media fun, at the expense of John Bonnett in particular, did not stop there, as a week later, on the 2nd October, the newspaper produced a continuation of the wedding story with a demand, supposedly from the mother of John Bonnett, that the story be retracted.

The newspaper began its apparent retraction by apologising for having shown a lack of judgement, a kind of 'temporary insanity', in printing the wedding announcement, which had first appeared in the *Lincolnshire Chronicle* on the previous Friday. In mock humility and disingenuous reassurance, the article insisted that the Lincoln newspaper, 'a highly respectable Conservative journal', was found in every clerical household in the country, which therefore made it a reliable authority on 'hymeneal matters'.

What followed was an alleged letter, sent in by Mrs Bonnett, which had been penned by her son, who had requested her to forward it to the newspaper for publication. The letter was a ludicrous disjointed compound of spluttering outrage and disgruntled accusation, written in broken grammar and syntax, which was clearly a parody of the speaking voice of the uneducated Lincolnshire countryman.

Should the interested or bewildered readers have had any doubts about the veracity of the source of the Horncastle wedding story, they would have been justified by looking back on the *Lincolnshire Chronicle* of Friday, 1st October.

There was a story relating to a man named Bonnett, employed at the Red Lion, in Boston, who had fallen into the Bargate Drain and had narrowly escaped drowning: whether this was John Bonnett of Fishtoft, it does not say.

Further, there was no mention of any wedding at Horncastle in the newspaper, other than that of Mr John Taylor Wing and Miss Clara Sheriff, at the Congregational Chapel.

The *Boston Guardian* had perpetrated a ridiculous hoax which entertained its readers for a couple of weeks and, at the same time, made its views on the acquittal of both Ellen Green and John Bonnett very obvious.

Appendix

Key Players In The Story Of Ellen Green

ALLEN, John. Farmer. House used for inquest into death of Thomas Green. Resident of Wythe Lane, Fishtoft.

ALLEN, Lucy. Wife of John Allen. Gave evidence at the trial of Ellen Green, at Lincoln Assizes. Resident of Wythe Lane, Fishtoft.

ALLENBY, Samuel. Served on Grand Jury at the trial of Ellen Green, at Lincoln Assizes. Resident of Cadwell Hall.

BAILES, W H. Solicitor. Defended John Bonnett at Boston Sessions House hearing. Resident of Boston.

BEAN, C. Solicitor. Prosecution Counsel at Boston Sessions House hearing.

BERGNE-COUPLAND, Richard Coupland. Served on Grand Jury at the trial of Ellen Green, at Lincoln Assizes. Resident of Skellingthorpe Hall.

BICKNELL, Captain Philip. Chief Constable of Lincolnshire. Attended hearing at Boston Sessions House.

BONNETT, John. Waggoner. Arrested on suspicion of the wilful murder of Thomas Green. Found Not Guilty. Gave evidence at trial of Ellen Green at Lincoln Assizes. Resident of Fishtoft.

CLEGG, Dr Walter. Coroner. Presided at inquest into death of Thomas Green. Gave evidence at the trial of Ellen Green, at Lincoln Assizes. Resident of Boston.

DALLISON, Maximillian H. Served on Grand Jury at the trial of Ellen Green, at Lincoln Assizes. Resident of Greetwell Hall. Manton.

DYER, Benjamin Bissell. Solicitor. Defended Ellen Green at Boston Sessions House hearing. Resident of Boston.

ELLISON, Richard George. Served on Grand Jury at the trial of Ellen Green, at Lincoln Assizes. Resident of Boultham Hall.

EMERIS, William Robert. Served on Grand Jury at the trial of Ellen Green, at Lincoln Assizes. Resident of Westgate, Louth.

FERRABY, John. Served on Grand Jury at the trial of Ellen Green, at Lincoln Assizes. Resident of Wootton Hall.

FINCH-HATTON, Honourable Murray Edward Gordon. Served on Grand Jury as Foreman at the trial of Ellen Green, at Lincoln Assizes. Resident of Haverholme Priory.

GARFIT, Thomas. Banker. Presiding magistrate with Lieutenant-Colonel Charles Moore at Boston Sessions House hearing. Resident of Skirbeck, Boston.

GLEED, Captain Richard. Served on Grand Jury at the trial of Ellen Green, at Lincoln Assizes. Resident of Park House, Donington.

GREEN, Ellen. Accused of the wilful murder of her husband, Thomas Green. Tried at Lincoln Assizes and found Not Guilty.

GREEN, George. Son of Thomas and Ellen Green. Gave evidence at inquest into death of Thomas Green, at Boston Sessions House hearing and trial of Ellen Green, at Lincoln Assizes, Resident of Fishtoft.

GREEN, Thomas. Cottager. Died of alleged arsenic poisoning. Resident of Fishtoft.

HENSON, Sergeant Thomas. Lincolnshire Constabulary. Gave evidence at Boston Sessions House hearing and at the trial of Ellen Green, at Lincoln Assizes. Resident of Boston.

HOPKINS, Frederick Lyon. Served on Grand Jury at the trial of Ellen Green, at Lincoln Assizes. Resident of Wide Bargate, Boston.

HUTTON, William. Served on Grand Jury at the trial of Ellen Green, at Lincoln Assizes. Resident of Gate Burton Hall.

LAWRANCE, John Compton. Counsel for the Defence at the trial of Ellen Green, at Lincoln Assizes. Resident of Dunsby Hall, Bourne.

LINDLEY, Baron Nathaniel. Presiding judge at trial of Ellen Green, at Lincoln Assizes.

LOWE, Dr George May. Lincolnshire County Analyst. Gave evidence at Boston Sessions House hearing and trial of Ellen Green, at Lincoln Assizes. Resident of 2 Cornhill, Lincoln.

LUARD, George Augustus. Served on Grand Jury at the trial of Ellen Green, at Lincoln Assizes. Resident of Blyborough Hall.

MASSINGBERD-MUNDY, Charles. Served on Grand Jury at the trial of Ellen Green, at Lincoln Assizes. Resident of Ormsby Hall.

MITCHELL, John. Labourer. Gave evidence at Boston Sessions House hearing and trial of Ellen Green, at Lincoln Assizes.

MOORE, John Thomas. Greengrocer. Gave evidence at Boston Sessions House hearing and trial of Ellen Green, at Lincoln Assizes. Resident of Boston.

MOORE, Lieutenant-Colonel Charles Thomas John. Presiding magistrate with Thomas Garfit at Boston Sessions House hearing. Served on Grand Jury at the trial of Ellen Green, at Lincoln Assizes. Resident of Frampton Hall.

NEVILLE, George. Served on Grand Jury at the trial of Ellen Green, at Lincoln Assizes. Resident of Stubton Hall.

PEACOCK, Edward. Served on Grand Jury at the trial of Ellen Green, at Lincoln Assizes. Resident of Bottesford Manor.

OSTLER, Eliza. Wife of John Ostler, cottager. Gave evidence at Boston Sessions House hearing and at the trial of Ellen Green, at Lincoln Assizes. Resident of Skirbeck.

OSTLER, John. Cottager. Gave evidence at Boston Sessions House hearing and trial of Ellen Green, at Lincoln Assizes. Resident of Skirbeck.

ROWSON, Esmeranda. Wife of Thomas Rowson, cottager. Gave evidence at inquest into death of Thomas Green, at Boston Sessions House hearing and trial of Ellen Green, at Lincoln Assizes, Resident of Boston.

STANILAND, Meaburn. Served on Grand Jury at the trial of Ellen Green, at Lincoln Assizes. Resident of Spilsby.

STEPHEN, James Fitzjames. Prosecuting Counsel at the trial of Ellen Green, at Lincoln Assizes.

STOPPER, Sarah. Sister of Ellen Green. Gave evidence at inquest into death of Thomas Green, at Boston Sessions House hearing and trial of Ellen Green, at Lincoln Assizes. Resident of Frieston.

STRINGER, Ann. Nurse. Gave evidence at Boston Sessions House hearing and trial of Ellen Green, at Lincoln Assizes. Resident of Boston.

SWAIN, Frederick. Gave evidence at Boston Sessions House hearing and trial of Ellen Green, at Lincoln Assizes, Resident of Skirbeck.

TAYLOR, Robert John. Served on Grand Jury at the trial of Ellen Green, at Lincoln Assizes. Resident of Burnham.

TROLLOPE, Arthur. Served on Grand Jury at the trial of Ellen Green, at Lincoln Assizes. Resident of Eastgate, Lincoln.

THORESBY, Superintendent. Gave evidence at Boston Sessions House hearing and trial of Ellen Green, at Lincoln Assizes.

TUXFORD, Dr Arthur. Surgeon. Gave evidence at inquest into death of Thomas Green, at Boston magistrates court and at trial of Ellen Green, at Lincoln Assizes. Resident of Pump Square, Boston.

TUXFORD, Dr James Edward. Surgeon. Performed post mortem on body of Thomas Green. Gave evidence at the inquest into the death of Thomas Green, at the Boston Sessions House hearing and at trial of Ellen Green, at Lincoln Assizes. Resident of Pump Square, Boston.

WELBY, John Earle. Served on Grand Jury at the trial of Ellen Green, at Lincoln Assizes. Resident of The Cottage, Allington.

WOOD, Elizabeth. Wife of John Wood, Foreman at Edward Porter's Frith Bank Farm. Gave evidence at Boston Sessions House hearing and trial of Ellen Green, at Lincoln Assizes.

WRIGHT, Samuel Wright. Served on Grand Jury at the trial of Ellen Green, at Lincoln Assizes. Resident of Brattleby Hall.

YATES, William. Gardener. Gave evidence at Boston Sessions House hearing and trial of Ellen Green, at Lincoln Assizes.

Bibliography

Archive sources

British Library

British Newspaper Digital Archive
(www.britishnewspaperarchive.co.uk)

Lincolnshire Archives

Prison Journal of John Nicholson, Governor
Ref: CoC 5/1/4:1848-1856
Prison Journal of James Foster, Governor
Ref: CoC 5/1//5/6: 1860-1868
Prison Journal of Ralph Howett, Surgeon
Ref: CoC 5/1/14, 1844-1849
Prison Journal of James Farr Broadbent, Surgeon

Ref: CoC 5/1/19, 1866-1878
Prison Journal of the Reverend Henry H W C Richter, Chaplain
Ref: CoC 5/1/21: 1839-1845
CoC 5/1/22: 1845-1850
CoC 5/1/27: 1866-1878

Directories

E R Kelly, *Directory of Lincolnshire with the Port of Hull and Neighbourhood with Map of the County*, various dates

William White, *History, Gazetteer, and the Directory of Lincolnshire and the City and Diocese of Lincoln*, various dates

Census Records

1841-1881

Newspapers

Jane Bell

Lincolnshire Chronicle, 4th April, 1845, p.2
Stamford Mercury, 4th April, 1845, p.3
Lincolnshire Chronicle, 11th April, 1845, p.3

Stamford Mercury, 11th April, 1845, p.3
Lincolnshire Chronicle, 18th April, 1845, p.3
Stamford Mercury, 18th April, 1845, p.3
Evening Mail, 24th July, 1845, p.4
Morning Herald, 24th July, 1845, p.7
The Sun, 24th July, 1845, p.5
Lincolnshire Chronicle, 25th July, 1845, p.2
Nottingham Review and General Advertiser for the Midland Counties, 25th July, p.5
Stamford Mercury, 25th July, 1845, p.2
Illustrated London News, 26th July, 1845, p.7
Liverpool Mercury, 2nd August, 1845, p.10
Manchester Courier and Lancashire General Advertiser, 3rd August, 1845, p.7

Elizabeth Dodds

Louth and North Lincolnshire Advertiser, 4th August, 1860, p.2
Stamford Mercury, 10th August, 1860, p.4
Lincolnshire Chronicle, 10th August, 1860, p.6
Louth and North Lincolnshire Advertiser, 11th August, 1860, p.3
Sleaford Gazette, 11th August, 1860, p.4
Newark Advertiser, 15th August, 1860, p.2
Lincolnshire Chronicle, 30th November, 1860, p.5
Sleaford Gazette, 1st December, 1860, p.4
The Express, 8th December, 1860, p.4

The Globe, 8th December, 1860, p.4
The Sun, 8th December, 1860, p.4
Lincolnshire Chronicle, 14th December, 1860, p.3
Stamford Mercury, 14th December, 1860, p.6
Cheltenham Mercury, 15th December, 1860, p.2
Hull Advertiser and Exchange Gazette, 15th December, 1860, p.10
Lancaster Gazette, 15th December, 1860, p.6
Louth and North Lincolnshire Advertiser, 15th December, 1860, p.4
Manchester Times, 15th December, 1860, p.6
Sleaford Gazette, 15th December, 1860, p.4
The Era, 16th December, 1860, p.9
Sleaford Gazette, 22nd December, 1860, p.4

Ellen Green

Boston Guardian and Lincolnshire Independent, 15th May, 1875, p.2
Lincolnshire Chronicle, 21st May, 1875, p.7
Boston Guardian and Lincolnshire Independent, 21st May, 1875, p.7
Grantham Journal, 22nd May, 1875, p.3
Lincolnshire Chronicle, 28th May, 1875, p.8
Stamford Mercury, 28th May, 1875, p.6
Lincolnshire Chronicle, 16th July, 1875, p.5
Stamford Mercury, 23rd July, 1875, pp.4,5
Lincolnshire Chronicle, 30th July, 1875, pp.5,6,7

Stamford Mercury, 30st July, 1875, p.7
Boston Guardian and Lincolnshire Independent, 31st July, p.4
Grantham Journal, 31st July, 1875, p.4
Sleaford Gazette, 31st July, 1875, p.4
Boston Guardian, 25th September, 1875, p.2
Boston Guardian, 2nd October, 1875, p.2

Books/Articles

Elizabeth Dodds

The Capital Punishment Commission; together with the Minutes of Evidence and Appendix, (Eyre and Spottiswood: London, 1866), p.259.

Katherine Watson, *Poisoned Lives, English Poisoners and their Victims*, (Hambledon and London, 2004), pp.36 and 72.

Internet Articles

Jane Bell

https:/www.grimsbytelegraph.cp.uk/newsw/nostalgia/suspected-murder-in-laceby-940697

General

The Capital Punishment Commission; together with the Minutes of Evidence and Appendix, (Eyre and Spottiswood: London, 1866)

Anderson, C L, *Lincolnshire Convicts to Australia, Bermuda and Gibraltar: a Study of Two Thousand Convicts*, (Laece Books: Lincoln, 1993)

Bentley, David, *English Criminal Justice in the Nineteenth-Century*, (Hambledon Press: London and Rio Grande, 1998)

Chamberlain, Mary, *Fenwomen*, (Virago Press: London, 1975)

Diamond, Michael, *Victorian Sensation, or the Spectacular, the Shocking and the Scandalous in Nineteenth-Century Britain*, (Anthem Press: London, 2003)

Flanders, Judith, *The Invention of Murder: How the Victorians Revelled in Death and Detection and Created Modern Crime*,(Harper Press: London, 2011)

Lewis, J R, *The Victorian Bar*, (Robert Hale: London, 1982)

Loudon, Irvine, *Medical Care and the General Practitioner, 1750-1850*, (Clarendon Press: Oxford, 1986)

Moyes, Malcolm, *By Force of Circumstances: the Lefley*

Case Reopened, (Matador: Kibworth Beauchamp, 2021)

ibid, *Attired in Deepest Mourning: Eliza Joyce, Mary Ann Milner and Priscilla Biggadike*, (Matador: Kibworth Beauchamp, 2022)

Olney, R J, *Lincolnshire Politics, 1832-1885*, (Oxford University Press: Oxford, 1973)

ibid, *Rural Society and County Government in Nineteenth-Century Lincolnshire*, (Lincoln: History of Lincolnshire Volume 10, 1979)

Robinson, Benjamin Coulson, *Bench and Bar, Reminiscences of One of the Last of an Ancient Race*, Hurst and Blackett Ltd: London, 1889)

Steinbach, Susie, *Women in England, 1760-1914: a Social History*, (Wiedenfeld & Nicholson: London, 2004)

Taylor, David, *Crime, Policing and Punishment, 1750-1914*, (MacMillan Press: London, 1998)

Ward, Arthur C, *Stuff and Silk*, (Gansey Publications: Ramsey, 1948)

Watson, Cassie, *Very Serious Pecuniary Loss and Inconvenience: A Jury's Plea* – posted on https://legalhistorymiscellany.com/2019/09/22/very-serious-pecuniary-loss-and inconvenience

Watson, Katherine, *Poisoned Lives, English Poisoners and their Victims*, (Hambledon and London, 2004)

Whorton, James C, *The Arsenic Century: how*

Victorian Britain was Poisoned at Home, Work and Play, (Oxford University Press: Oxford, 2010)

Williams, Montague, *Leaves of a Life: being the Reminiscences of the Life of Montague Williams*, (Houghton Mifflin & Co: Boston and New York, 1890), 2 volumes